THE MAKING OF A PARA

SIDGWICK & JACKSON
LONDON

THE MAKING
OF A
PARA

Rory Bridson

First published in Great Britain in 1989
by Sidgwick & Jackson Limited

ISBN 0-283-99918-7

Printed in West Germany by Mohndruck Limited for
Sidgwick & Jackson Limited
1 Tavistock Chambers, Bloomsbury Way
London WC1A 2SG

Design: Graham Bingham and Simon Bleeze

Additional material: Chris Marshall

Editorial: John Boteler

The members of The Parachute Regiment and
5 Airborne Brigade who have helped are too numerous
for all to be mentioned by name, but those who have
been particulary helpful include: Richard Brinton,
Peter Kennedy, Andy Warner, Johnathan Shaw,
Chip Chapman, John Gallagher, Peter Wall,
Bill Hayward, Rupert Pritchard, Alan Morris and
Geoff Norton.

My special thanks to: the staff of 'P' Company;
C Company 1 PARA; 2 PARA; B Company 3 PARA;
4 Company 10 PARA; Depot the Parachute Regiment
and Airborne Forces; No 1 Parachute Training School,
RAF Brize Norton; PCAU.

Thanks also for the hospitality shown me by the various
Officers' Messes.

I would also like to thank Peter MacDonald, for all his
help with the text and pictures.

**Front cover and frontispiece: Soldiers from 2 PARA
with SA 80s.
Back cover: A battalion drop onto Denmark during a
Nato exercise.**

CONTENTS

PREFACE

What manner of men are these who wear the maroon beret?

They are, firstly, all volunteers, and are toughened by hard physical training. As a result, they have that infectious optimism and that offensive eagerness which come from physical well-being.

They have jumped from the air and, by doing so, have conquered fear.

Their duty lies in the van of battle: they are proud of their honour, and have never failed in any task.

They have the highest standards in all things, whether it be skill in battle or smartness in execution of all peacetime duties.

They have shown themselves to be as tenacious and determined in defence as they are courageous in attack.

They are, in fact, men apart.

Every man an emperor.

Field Marshal Montgomery of Alamein

These words, though said so many years ago, still hold true today — as The Parachute Regiment showed in the Falklands on the rocky slopes of Mount Longdon and the naked peatlands around Darwin and Goose Green. But what does it take to be a Paratrooper, to earn the Red Beret and join one of the world's élite regiments? I hope that the following pages will do something to answer that question.

In writing this book I have been unashamedly biased — as a Territorial Army member of the Regiment I could not be otherwise. For Regimental pride is fierce within all its members. Even so, I hope my judgments are balanced.

Although The Parachute Regiment and 5 Airborne Brigade have given me every assistance in preparing this text, the views expressed are entirely my own or those of the people interviewed. They do not necessarily reflect official Regimental or Army policy.

Sergeant O'Kane ('P' Company instructor) having a few quiet words at the end of the '10-miler'.

THE MAROON MACHINE

What makes a paratrooper different? What gives British Paras the drive and fighting power that have taken them to victory all over the world — from the freezing rain of the Falklands to the baking rocks of South Arabia? There is no doubt that a soldier has to have something a little bit different to be a Para. He has to show aggression, and be able to display the famed Airborne Initiative.

The most obvious distinction between The Parachute Regiment and other British infantry regiments is the paratrooper's disconcerting habit of jumping out of perfectly serviceable aircraft. But this is not the most important difference. To the Regiment, a parachute is just a means of getting into battle — albeit a very dramatic one. What matters is what the Airborne Soldier does once he hits the ground, and that depends on his character and his training. For it is the consistent quality of the individual paratrooper that separates The Parachute Regiment from the rest.

This high quality is needed throughout the Regiment because of the very nature of airborne operations. The peculiar characteristics of the paratrooper's battlefield

Aspiring Toms going over the bridge at the start of the '10-miler' — the main event on Monday morning of the Aldershot phase of 'P' Company.

A lance-corporal of 2 PARA during a break in a training exercise using live rounds. Note the fixed bayonet on his IW (Individual Weapon), a member of the SA 80 family.

have shaped the whole ethos of the Regiment, and given it a regimental spirit and attitude that have kept it in the world's élite since its creation. If a nation is to go to the expense and military complexity of dropping men behind enemy lines and supplying them from the air, then their task must be very important — usually out of all proportion to the size of the unit involved. So every member of the Regiment must realise that the only thing that matters to The Parachute Regiment is the mission itself.

The element of surprise is vital for the lightly equipped Airborne Soldier

Because of the emphasis on fulfilling the mission, The Parachute Regiment attaches great importance to determination — determination to achieve the mission on the part of everyone in the Regiment. Perhaps the most well-known example of this in recent times was that of Lieutenant-Colonel 'H' Jones who, during the Falklands campaign, was killed when he charged and took out an Argentinian machine-gun nest single-handed, for which action he was posthumously awarded the Victoria Cross. And the Regiment's most famous action was at Arnhem in 1944, when the 1st Airborne Division, tasked with taking and holding the bridge over the Rhine, virtually wiped itself out fighting an élite SS Panzer Corps.

Actually achieving the mission usually requires considerable aggression. Even to perform the very unnatural act of leaping out of an aircraft into empty space requires each paratrooper to summon up aggression within himself to overcome his fear. Once on the ground, the element of surprise is vital for the lightly equipped Airborne Soldier coming up against an often numerically superior enemy. In order to utilise that surprise to the full, and to capture the objective before enemy reinforcements can arrive, every member of the Regiment must have the aggressiveness required for instant, shock action. Often, a paratrooper may come under fire even as he lands on the

DZ (Dropping Zone), and then aggression is required just to get a firm 'foothold' on the ground.

This is how a member of 3 PARA describes it: 'Our troops are more aggressive than any other troops anyway, and it all boils down to the training and the type of guy needed to pass that training. We find that the aggression amongst our blokes is very high; they are very aggressive.'

Every parachute jump is the equivalent of eight hours work

Just as aggression is a vital component in a soldier's armoury, so too is fitness. Military parachuting is, after all, very hard work. According to medical experts, every parachute jump is the equivalent of eight hours work in terms of the mental and physical stress it induces. The preparation before a jump is considerable. Each paratrooper is briefed, both on what he needs to know for the drop, and also on what he needs to know in order to achieve his mission once he is on the ground. He must draw and fit his parachute and practise the drills he needs to rendezvous with the other members of his company after landing. He may get very little sleep if all this takes place just before the jump. Once in the aircraft, he may doze, but up to 20 minutes before leaping through the door, he has to stand up with all his equipment on. With a main parachute, a reserve chute and all the weapons, ammunition and food he needs for the forthcoming operation, this can amount to as much as 80kg. In a bucking aircraft flying just above the tree tops, this is a strenuous task — made even worse if the man is feeling airsick. The tension and anxiety involved in parachuting, and the aggression needed to actually throw himself through the aircraft door, sap his energy even further.

Airborne operations have a habit of not going according to plan

Furthermore, once he hits the ground, the Para's job has only just begun. He must use the effect of surprise and move quickly to attack his target before the enemy can react to the parachute assault. The target is often several miles from the DZ, and the Para is heavily loaded with all his weapons and equipment. There are never enough aircraft to drop all but a small number of specialist vehicles, so he must walk. And walk fast, or 'tab' as it is known in the Regiment. When he gets to his objective, he then has to attack it and take it from the enemy. He may then have to defend it for days, beating off what may be incessant enemy counter-attacks.

Being complex and difficult undertakings, airborne operations have a habit of not going according to plan.

Life for a Para is not all hard work. R&R (Rest and Recreation) after Exercise Caltrop Force — held in the United States in 1989 — gave the members of 1 PARA a welcome opportunity to see some of the spectacular sights of the western USA.

This can be due to the ground forces not linking up in time (or even at all, as happened occasionally during World War II). It can be due to the weather delaying reinforcements or resupply, or it can be due to the aircraft dropping men in the wrong place. A further factor is the enemy, which has an annoying tendency to interfere in even the most well-planned operation.

Both aggression and initiative must be channelled in the right direction

It is no accident that the motto of The Parachute Regiment is *Utrinque Paratus* — 'Ready for Anything'. For the Regiment must at all times be flexible, and every member must be able to adapt instantly to the situation in which he finds himself and act accordingly. To do this requires intelligence and initiative, not just from the officers and NCOs, but from the Toms as well. (A 'Tom' is a private soldier in The Parachute Regiment.) In a drop, companies, platoons and sections may well be widely scattered. Private soldiers may be separated from their commanders and find themselves in the middle of enemy territory in a totally different area from where they had been briefed to land. In the D-Day drop in the early hours of 6 June 1944, for example, over 1000 men of the 6th Airborne Division were scattered far and wide, miles from their battalions. Even so, as they struggled through marshes and bogs to get back to their units, they managed to cause destruction and confusion to German

forces along the way and create the impression of a much larger airborne landing.

This risk of chaos in all parachute operations is why the Regiment encourages a mixture of cunning, drive, intelligence and applied common sense in all its members. It has even given this requirement a special name — ABI, or Airborne Initiative.

Both aggression and initiative must be channelled in the right direction if they are to have maximum effect, so a Parachute Regiment soldier must be not only a disciplined, but also a thinking soldier — one who can make suggestions as well as obey orders.

In an airborne operation there is no turning back

A section commander in the Falklands describes his own experience concerning his men's initiative during the conflict: 'I could formulate a plan in my own mind, but a private soldier can often see better. So, although I am issuing that plan and they will stick to it rigidly if necessary, if they can see a better route up or a better position to attack from, then they will come out with it. They wouldn't just say "Yes", and then just do it like wooden-tops [Guardsmen] would. Of course, they wouldn't just say "Oh no, I don't agree with this" either; but they are sensible and they think about it. They may have been lying 200-300 metres away from me and have actually seen a good, solid piece of cover, and therefore that may change your plan and you think, "Well yes, good bit of advice, son", and do it his way. They think because they don't want to get killed.'

If there is no one around to give him orders, then the average Tom will make up his own mind and act accordingly. A SNCO (Senior Non-Commissioned Officer) from 2 PARA describes the reactions of his private soldiers: 'If somebody shouts something, then they will do it — but not mindlessly. In the Falklands, where a section commander had been killed or wounded, then a private soldier ran that small part of the battle...they are capable of thinking for themselves. By the same token, they also do as they are told.'

In an airborne operation there is no turning back. Once a paratrooper has leapt through the door, he can't simply turn round, get back on the aircraft and go home — he is committed. Miles behind enemy lines, heavily outnumbered and with the element of surprise so important, an airborne force has to succeed first time. If it fails to achieve its mission, it can not 'go back and try again

tomorrow', as is often possible in conventional operations.

Because of this, The Parachute Regiment places great emphasis on professionalism, at all levels. It has no monopoly on this quality — the British Army as a whole is one of the most professional in the world, and in any other army most of the British line infantry battalions would be considered élite, such is their professionalism. But The Parachute Regiment has the added incentive of no second chances.

A final characteristic of the Parachute Regiment soldier, and one that is also due to his airborne role, is his strong self-reliance. Actual airlift capacity is always limited in an airborne operation, so a paratrooper must rely on his legs for transport, and on what he carries to survive and fight — at least initially. This is one reason why Parachute Regiment soldiers were so well-suited to the rigours of the Falklands conflict, where transport out of the beachhead was so very limited. The Airborne Soldier knows that the aircraft bringing his supplies may not arrive, that they may be shot down, or even drop their loads in the wrong place. So he carries extra food and ammunition in his bergen (rucksack) and is prepared to go and get what he needs for himself, to requisition transport, to acquire ammunition and food. This often requires ABI — another reason why initiative is encouraged in the Regiment.

The outcome of battle rests far more on the shoulders of the individual Tom

The paratrooper must also be self-reliant when he fights. Any fire support he receives must be flown in, so he can never get as much as the conventional soldier. Unlike his colleague in BAOR (British Army of the Rhine) in West Germany, when the Airborne Infantryman gets into trouble, he cannot simply call down the corps artillery, nor can he rely on a neighbouring brigade to stop the enemy from outflanking him. With much fewer support weapons, The Parachute Regiment relies a lot less on material and technology. In an airborne operation, the outcome of battle rests far more on the shoulders of the individual Tom.

These are the reasons why The Parachute Regiment demands a high standard of its soldiers, the special circumstances that have forged the ethos of the Regiment. To get the right kind of person with all these qualities is a difficult task. An interview or medical inspection will not bring them out. So, ever since its creation in World War II, The Parachute Regiment has tested the fitness and strength of character of everyone who wants to be a Para. It does this in a gruelling selection procedure that pushes all who go through it to their limits — the legendary 'P' Company.

A recruit on 'P' Company has his blisters syringed during one of the endurance marches of Exercise Steel Bayonet, held in the Brecon Beacons.

NO PAIN NO GAIN

Ten miles in one hour and 45 minutes carrying 20kg; a seven-mile race over Welsh mountains helping to carry a 75kg stretcher — these are just two of the events of 'P' Company, tests that push a potential Para to the limits of pain and endurance, and beyond.

'P' Company is hard. Any test designed to bring out the qualities required of an Airborne Soldier has to be. Few people in civilian life today have ever had to run with a large weight on their backs and heavy boots on their feet or, indeed, even had the opportunity to put their endurance and determination to such a test. To put volunteers straight from 'civvy street' through the selection procedure that sets the minimum standards of the Parachute Regiment soldier is unrealistic and would result in only a very small percentage passing. So, a new recruit to the Regiment spends 12 weeks building himself up, both physically and mentally, for 'P' company itself, the gruelling week of tests that will decide if he has what it takes to become a Para.

The agony of Test Week. A Para medic attached to 'P' Company administers a dose of 'Tincbenco' to a recruit in order to draw out his blisters so that he may continue.

Most of those 12 weeks are spent at The Depot, The Parachute Regiment and Airborne Forces. This is situated in Browning Barracks, Aldershot. The staff at the Depot that deal with the raw recruits are divided into two companies — Recruit, or 'R' Company, which is responsible for teaching each new intake, and Pegasus, or 'P' Company, which includes the staff who test all those who wish to join The Parachute Regiment or Airborne Forces.

'R' Company has the initial contact with all the aspiring paratroopers who have come straight from 'civvy street' to join as private soldiers, and overall responsibility for the 23 weeks of basic training, even when the recruits are going through 'P' Company or parachute training. The men who see the most of the recruits during this period are the corporals; they command and train their own sections of 'crows', as recruits are known in The Parachute Regiment, 'Joe Crow' being the personification of the recruit.

A motley collection of Rockers, Bikers and Disco Dancers

The first week of recruit training is when 'Joe Civilian' and the Regiment get to know one another. It is often hard to tell which gets the bigger shock, especially in the case of a corporal who has just been posted to the Depot from his battalion. These corporals are some of the most experienced in the Regiment, and, before being posted to the Depot for two years, may have already been with their battalions for six or seven. After so long in the Army, it usually comes as a real eye-opener the first time they see what the members of the rest of society are really like.

It is at Aldershot railway station that the fresh-faced civilian first meets the Regiment. It is not hard to spot new recruits for the Army as soon as they get off the train from London. They may not yet have the short hair and confident posture of a 'squaddie', but their armfuls of bags and their nervous looks of bewilderment give away their destination as clearly as any baggage label.

Once the corporals have ticked off 'John' and 'Mark' on their long list of names, they then have to explain to the new arrivals that no, they can't have their 'guns' yet, and no, they are not going parachuting tomorrow.

Back at Depot, the recruits make their first attempt to form up into some semblance of a military formation, and the two sides get a chance to 'eye each other up'. 'Joe Crow' sees men with an enormous variety of badges on wrist, arm or shoulder, and who seem to be of various higher levels of importance, but who all wear what he wants to wear — the Red Beret. To the staff, this new platoon is a motley collection of Rockers, Bikers and Disco Dancers, with hair lengths ranging from Skinhead to Hippie, and dress sense varying from Leathers to War on Want.

The first step in turning this diverse cross-section of society into a cohesive team that works together is to emphasise the unit rather than the individual, and this is achieved initially by making all the recruits look the same, or at least as similar as possible. A two-minute trip to the barber removes the carefully nurtured locks, and the now severely cropped hair reveals just who was hiding his scrawny neck or protruding ears — features which, by the time he finishes recruit training, 'Joe' will wish he never had.

In addition to getting their hair cut, the recruits spend the first two days of their training having medicals, filling in forms, and collecting kit. Already, they are beginning to discover how much the Army loves signatures, and how important it is to look after clothing and equipment. With the words, 'You sign, you lose, you pay', they begin to learn how much their own bit of illegible scrawl matters. For the recruits, getting their uniforms is usually an exciting time, suddenly turning them from civilians into soldiers. In the Regiment's eyes, of course, it will take a little longer. Simply wearing a uniform doesn't make the recruits into paratroopers, and, instead of the distinctive Red Beret of the Airborne Soldier, they have to wear 'combat caps', peaked caps made out of disruptive pattern material (DPM — camouflage). These are known as 'craphats' by the recruits, as a measure of their desire to be rid of them, and to become a full member of the Regiment and wear the coveted Red Beret. But first they have to earn it.

Not all of the new recruits decide they want to, though. In the words of a field officer at the Depot:

'Lots leave of their own volition within a couple of weeks, because they realise that they have done the wrong thing. They are allowed the "discharge by right", which is laid down in a parliamentary statute. Up until Week Eight, they can leave for only £100, which is just a nominal administrative fee. Thereafter, though, they are committed to their three-, six- or nine-year engagement. They can still leave, but to do so they have to spend a lot more money to buy themselves out.'

Even by the beginning of Day Two, the Depot staff have to deal with such 'time-wasters' — those that have 'made a mistake', that have quickly discovered that they and the Army 'do not get on', or for whom 'it's not really "me", corporal'.

Some of the recruits have never left home before and, as one of the Depot staff put it: 'For many of them, their mothers make their beds, and tea has always been on the table. They have never even picked up an iron.'

Many of the recruits, even those who have come straight from such a pampered home life, will not necessarily want to leave. They rise to the challenges of the new way of life, realising that they are the only ones who are going to look after their accommodation, their kit and themselves. Others, however, unused to the mundane chores of being a soldier, are not prepared to put up with them — the novelty of wearing a uniform soon wears off when the recruit discovers he has to press it every day. As one warrant officer at Depot put it: 'They have to change, their attitude has to change, or they will never get through the system.'

'You have to maintain the momentum all the way through'

Others who drop out at this early stage do so because all they want is to be a 'ruffty, tuffty paratrooper', and jump out of aeroplanes. The fact that they will have to wait several months to do so causes some to leave straight away, rather than 'see the thing through'. In the opinion of one senior officer at the Depot:

'Personally, I think they are impatient, and that is part of modern life today. They want to be a parachutist immediately and can hardly wait two or three weeks, and so

you have to maintain the momentum all the way through.'

It is not just the impatience of the recruits that strikes the Recruit Company staff. Before they join, many have little knowledge of the Regiment and the training process — while some expect to be parachuting in the first week, others expect to be off to some sunny clime as soon as they join the Regiment.

The most entertaining surprise for the instructors comes at the end of Week One. They tell the recruits to pack their bergens for a night in the field, and even the most experienced corporals never cease to be amazed by the slippers, pyjamas and pillows which appear that evening. Only by sheer hard work, patience and time do the staff succeed in turning such raw civilians into soldiers.

The first four weeks of training are taken up with the subjects any recruit is taught on joining the Army. These

Little do they know...Brand new recruits arriving at Depot PARA, Aldershot. Before them lie the months of training that will turn them from 'civvies' into paratroopers.

are: drill; weapons training — how to load and unload the SA 80 family of weapons, how to fire them, and what to do if they jam; who to salute and who not to salute; what each badge means; and what to call the different ranks. 'Joe Crow' is also taught the history of the Regiment — the important dates, people and places since Airborne Forces were formed in 1940 — and who is who and what their role is, both at the Depot and in the Regiment as a whole.

'If you can't take a joke, you shouldn't have joined'

It may seem strange that such a forward-looking, modern regiment as the Paras devotes time in its very tight training programme to history. But it is important to let the new recruit learn about the tradition of excellence; to show him what the Airborne Soldier has achieved in the past and what he is expected to be capable of in the future. It helps to make him want to join the Regiment, to pass through all his recruit training and 'P' Company, to feel that he belongs to a 'good outfit'.

Any such encouragement to motivation takes on

Recruit training continues in all weathers — regardless. Here a 'crow' empties water from his boot after a wet day on the Steeplechase. By Test Week he will be able to complete two circuits of the 1.3km course in around 17.5 minutes.

Recruits on sick parade, with essential kit in their packs in case they are admitted. Note the despised 'craphats', and the red shoulder flashes denoting Retraining Platoon.

added importance because of the stress of Depot. For a recruit, life at the Depot is a time of considerable mental, as well as physical, stress. 'Joe' soon finds out why food in the Regiment is called 'scoff' — the only way to eat enough of it to keep you going is to do just that, 'scoff' it. With such a tight training programme, the time available for meals is the bare minimum. The sooner 'Joe' has to be back, the longer the queue at the cookhouse, or so it seems, and that often leaves the new recruit about four minutes to get his meal 'down his neck' and get to wherever he has to be next, along with whatever kit he needs.

Each day seems to last for ever, except Sunday, which is a rest day and over in a flash. On the other days, there is very little time to relax, with reveille at 0700 hours and a packed training programme until the recruits are 'stood down' at 2000 hours. In that 13-hour period, if 'Joe' is not attending a lesson, then whatever he's doing he's got to do in 'double-quick' time, whether it's eating, washing, or preparing for the next period. The pressure on the recruit is intense and constant. But, 'If you can't take a joke, you shouldn't have joined.'

What 'spare' time 'Joe' has is spent cleaning accommodation, polishing boots, and washing and pressing kit.

But the rooms can always be cleaner, and the creases that bit sharper. So, as an officer from Depot puts it:

'We actually have a compulsory lights-out now; we have to, because they're so keen that they will go on unless we say: "Now, lights out." Unless they get their food and rest, they are not going to make it through the first week. We are very conscious that food and rest is putting back what we take out.'

Piled on top of the mental stress of the pressure of Depot comes the physical stress of increased fitness training. With the 'real knackers' out of the way, the build-up to 'P' Company can now begin. The runs start to get longer and longer, and the recruits — encouraged, as ever, by the instructors — fight to get that little bit more from their heaving lungs and aching legs. As the build-up progresses, 'Joe Crow' has to give maximum effort — not just for 10 minutes, but for 40 or 50.

As the Depot staff struggle to improve the fitness and

Candidates on an All-Arms 'P' Company double on the spot after returning from an eight-mile battle march, carrying bergens but no weapons. The officers on PPS wear white PT vests.

determination of the recruits, their biggest battle is with the modern way of life. If you are not used to hot and cold running water and gas central heating, living in the field does not seem such a discomfort. Also, if you have accepted discipline from parents, schoolmasters and at work, then it is much easier to accept discipline from corporals and sergeant-majors. However, the ever-increasing

'cushiness' of the British life-style, with all its 'mod cons', and the lack of discipline in society, mean that today's recruit gets more of a shock when he joins the Army than did his father or grandfather. But if a recruit really wants to join the Regiment (and for the right reasons), then he will adapt to this changing way of life.

What is more difficult to overcome for both instructors and recruits is the physiology of the human product of the modern way of life. Compared with the recruit of even six or seven years ago, today's recruit needs far more knocking into shape to become a soldier — let alone a Parachute Regiment soldier.

Yet many of the young recruits entering the Regiment are still able to find the mental attitude required to overcome their fitness problems, to keep going in the face of adversity. A senior officer from the Depot describes the fitness problems faced by modern recruits:

'We do find that the young man coming in now is, at the same time, both under-nourished and somewhat spoon-fed. With less competitive sport being played at school, he is weaker in some ways than he was before. But, from somewhere in his mind, you can still get the same attributes out of him. It's still there, as he is fundamentally the same man. But it *is* a very sharp shock to the system when he arrives.'

'More important than their physical hardness is their mental attitude'

This officer blames the problem on a lack of 'decent nourishment. There is no doubt about it; when you see a chap of 17 or 18 who has been fed on junk food, he can be a rather weedy specimen. Structurally, he is OK; but you have to work on him, you really have — heart and lungs. They are suffering at the age of 17 and 18 from not being fit in heart or lungs, and we have to be very careful with them. We don't let them run in boots until the fifth week; they are now issued with 'Puma' running shoes and so on. We have to be very careful as we get an awful lot of what are called stress fractures, induced marching fractures. We have a lot of tendonitis in the back of the heel, because the young man has never worn a leather-soled shoe in his life, and that comes as quite a shock. There are lots of little things like that.

'But more important than their physical hardness is their mental attitude, and I think, quite honestly, that the best of the youth today is as good, if not better, than it has ever been. And the best are very motivated, have got a lot of character, a lot of tenacity, and it's these sort of quali-

Boots Combat High and blisters go together during the Wales Phase of Test Week. In the absence of a bullet, this officer bites on his combat scarf during a foot inspection.

Foreign paras may try their luck on Test Week when visiting. Here a Canadian paratrooper is given a welcome drink by a member of the 'P' Company staff during the Wales Phase.

ties that we're really looking for, because they respond extremely well to training, and they enjoy their training. They'll keep ahead of the game, and as long as they can do that, then they're going to make it.'

While the design of the early models of the Army's 'Boots, Combat, High' may have something to do with the high incidence of tendonitis in recruits, the feeling that the young men of today are not as fit as in the past is not restricted to The Parachute Regiment. The rest of the Army and the police force have also been alarmed by this deterioration in the fitness of the young men 'straight off the street'. They have measured this drop over the last six or seven years in their fitness entrance tests, so it is more than just fond memories of 'the good old days'.

With a lower standard of fitness on entering the Depot but with the same length of time — 12 weeks — before 'P' Company, today's recruit has to work a lot harder than

his predecessors did to come up to the standard of Pre-Parachute Selection. The intense pressure of Depot is, in itself, a form of selection before 'P' Company. It prepares the recruit for his time as a fully-fledged member of a battalion, when there may be one exercise after the other. Those who cannot take this strain during training, or lack the motivation to endure it, drop out.

The only way to survive is through teamwork. Camaraderie within the section quickly builds up because all the recruits are going through a difficult experience together. And, precisely because they are together for so much of the day, and under pressure for most of that time, they soon get to know each other really well. As most recruit platoons also live in eight-man rooms (partitioned into two four-man areas), there is very little of their character that they can hide from each other.

The 'midwife' to the birth of this team spirit is the section commander. As one of the Depot staff puts it:

'It starts from the fact that they are living together in a close environment, and they are not going to get the barrack block cleaned up and tidy unless it is done as a team.

There is an awful lot of help that has to come from within. The NCO instructors in the first four weeks will spend almost every night in the barrack block. We do have an NCO on duty every night until lights out — rather like a boarding school — so he is always there to give advice and help and so on. But after that, it is down to the platoon.'

This 'small unit bond' is even more important in combat than in training

The Depot staff also encourage team spirit through competition between sections. By telling each section how it compares with the others in the platoon, they help both to bind the section together and to improve the performance of the recruits.

However, the most important function of a good section spirit is in making a recruit want to stay in training and to overcome all the hurdles along the way, together with his mates. Of course, if he does not fit in with the rest of the section, and pull his weight as a member of the team, then he begins to feel that he does not belong, either in the section or in the Regiment. If the rest of the section enjoys a good team spirit, then he feels even more of an outsider. Such a recruit is much more likely to 'jack' (give up) when the pressure is on as he has less incentive than the others to stay the course.

In a way, this is another aspect of the selection process, almost a form of 'self-selection'. For if a recruit can't fit in with his peers at Depot, then he is very unlikely to fit in with a battalion. Both he and the Regiment are then better off if he is somewhere else. For this 'small unit bond' is even more important in combat than in training. In a shooting war, it is not just pain and effort that a soldier must expend for the sake of his mates in the section. It is often his life as well.

A good team spirit within the section can also help a recruit in a more direct way. If he is struggling, be it on a run or pressing his kit in time or whatever, then the other members of the section will help him out or encourage

A 'P'Company instructor from 7 (Para) RHA leads the way up the steep side of Pen-y-Fan in Wales. Although most of the 'P' Company staff are from the Regiment, one is always from other another unit of 5 Airborne Brigade.

him. If he is forever in need of help, however, then he will be unable to help out others when *they* need it, and unable to pull his weight as part of the team. Everyone else in the section soon starts to get fed up with the minimal amount he contributes to the group compared with how much he takes from it. Before long, he is left to founder on his own. The instructors adopt the same approach. In the words of one of the staff at the Depot:

'The strong will live and the weak will die. What we are really saying is that we will put the effort into those that are going to make it, and quite rightly.'

Sooner or later, almost every recruit goes through a 'bad patch' in his training. Nothing seems to be going right, the pressure of Depot is getting to be too much, and depression is creeping in. It is then that a section with a good spirit will cheer up and encourage their down-hearted friend and help him to 'get back up there' on top of the training with the desire to carry on. But in the end, it is only 'Joe' himself who can drag himself out of the jaws of failure, stimulated by the thought of those who had succumbed earlier on in the course. Again, this is almost a system of self-selection. An Airborne operation is usually a risky venture, with a lot that can go wrong. Behind enemy lines, often with the odds stacked against him, the paratrooper needs to be able to take disaster after disaster in his stride, to face each one, and then carry on fighting to achieve the mission.

Kit inspections are often a good test of whether or not 'Joe' is able to 'get back up there'. He has to iron his uniform carefully, including the items he is not wearing, and arrange everything neatly in his locker. When the platoon sergeant then throws a carefully pressed shirt out of the window and into the pouring rain, bellowing: 'Next time, turn the f—ing iron on!', it is undoubtedly only a matter of minutes before the next kit inspection. Such 'mini-disasters' seem to suddenly pile on top of one another, and it takes a resilient spirit, a considerable sense of humour, and a certain philosophical attitude to overcome them and carry on with the training.

If a recruit is struggling with training and finding it difficult to keep his head above water, then 'R' Company has a system to help him out. Once every few weeks, all the platoon staff attend a conference on how the 'crows' are coping with the course. The section commanders, platoon sergeant, and platoon commander discuss each recruit in turn to decide which, if any, should not continue on to the next training stage. The platoon commander has the final say, but he listens closely to his NCOs — particularly the poor performer's section commander. If 'Joe' is not up to scratch, then he has to go through that section of the train-

A bad case of 'bergen burns', made worse by coming on top of sunburn.

ing again. To do this he is 'back-squadded' — placed in the next platoon back that is going through Depot, usually four to six weeks behind his own. This is dreaded by the recruits, not only because of the extra time they will have to spend at Depot or the frustration of having to repeat the lessons, but also because they are separated from their mates in their section and platoon. They will have to fit in to a totally new group with its own spirit, make new friends and gain the trust of that group. The continual turnover of back-squadding, of Junior Paras coming in at Week Six, and of recruits coming in from other platoons, does not help the team spirit within the sections, which in consequence might not achieve stability until only two or three weeks before 'P' Company.

An alternative to immediate back-squadding is the Retraining, or Falklands Platoon, particularly if the recruit is injured, or if his fitness is not up to scratch. Those recruits who fail Pre-Parachute Selection also go into Falklands Platoon (itself a part of 'P' Company), until they are ready to take the test again.

At the end of Week Four, the recruits 'pass off the square'. This is a test of their drill (the 'square' being the drill square), their turn-out, and also their regimental knowledge, past and present. With this first stage in their training completed, they are starting to show the first signs of thinking, and acting, like soldiers. Their confidence is growing, and they are working better as a team — the section and platoon spirit is getting stronger. Or it should be.

Basic Wales also involves three days of adventure training

At this stage, the recruits are usually given a leave for the weekend — the first time they are allowed off camp in their free time since they arrived. But it has been known for this to be refused, and for a platoon to be confined to barracks instead. If the platoon staff feel that a lot of recruits want to 'jack', then they don't want to expose them to the soft comforts of home, and to 'understanding' family and friends who may encourage them to leave. The instructors would rather they spent the time with the other recruits, reinforcing friendships and building up a team spirit that might be lacking.

Nevertheless, most recruits, though glad of the break, are keen to continue with the course. For the next phase is about 'real' training — exercises in the field and shooting on the ranges, rather than the drill and locker inspections that they've had until now. And 'real' soldiering is what they all joined for.

But the first night's freezing hour on 'stag' (sentry duty) soon puts paid to any illusions a recruit might have about soldiering in the field. With the 'Hollywood Image' fast disappearing, the platoon staff begin to build up in the recruits a professional pride that gets its satisfaction from doing a job properly, even though that job may, at times, be unpleasant or monotonous.

Part of this period of 'individual training' (teaching the skills every soldier needs to know, rather than the particular skills of the infantry), is spent near Brecon, and it is known as 'Basic Wales'. The recruits learn how to camouflage themselves, how to move without being seen or heard, how to judge the distance to a target, and all the other basic skills a soldier must master before he can take his place in a section.

Besides three days of skills training, Basic Wales also involves three days of adventure training. As well as building up the recruits' characters, the 17-mile 'tabs' (Regimental slang for a march or run) introduce them to the hills, hills and more hills that they will come to know very well during 'P' Company. And for 'Joe', 'P' Company is on him all too soon. Once back from Wales, he spends some more time at Aldershot on basic skills, drill, and preparation for PPS. Then, after shooting for a week on the ranges at Lydd in Sussex and Hythe in Kent, it's back

to Aldershot again for checking on skills, and then comes the big test itself — 'P' Company.

However, Parachute Regiment recruits are not the only ones who attempt 'P' Company. Officers joining the Regiment, and all ranks in the rest of 5 Airborne Brigade who volunteer for parachute training, must also go through an 'All-Arms PPS' course.

This is a three week course, of which the last week — 'Test Week' — is the same as the recruits' 'P' Company week. Some of those recruits attempting the All-Arms course will have also done the All-Arms Commando Course, but the two are quite different. A gunner from 148 Battery, who has done both courses, compares them:

'The physical side of 'P' Company is a lot more intense than what they do on the Commando course. That's spread over 15 weeks, whereas 'P' Company is done in only two and a half.'

Also, although the Commando course involves carrying heavier weights over longer distances, it is done at a slower pace. As one 'P' Company CSM puts it:

'The Marine course is designed for them, for their particular type of animal. We want a nasty, aggressive, dirty little swine to stick bayonets into people, and therefore our course is geared for that type of thing — fast, furious, aggressive.'

Recruits negotiate the water on the Steeplechase. On cold winter mornings, the ice often has to be broken first.

What makes the All Arms PPS such a test is that it is a solid three weeks of unmitigated pain, of 10- and 14-mile tabs. By the start of Test Week, all the aspiring Airborne Soldiers are totally exhausted.

To prepare for this, certain units in 5 Airborne Brigade organise a three-week 'beat-up' period to improve their men's fitness. But even this requires training for. The CSM again: 'There are some people who spend three months in preparation before they actually get here — and they need it. The people that don't prepare will fail.'

The first hurdle to overcome is the Steeplechase

Those that lack motivation will also fail. And for the non-Parachute Regiment students on an All-Arms PPS, this is often more difficult than for the actual Para recruits. Many of the non-Paras do not have the prospect of gaining the famous Red Beret to make them push themselves that little bit extra, since several of the supporting units in 5 Airborne Brigade present the Red Beret to their men as soon as they are posted to the Brigade. Even so, many of the men from these units who then go on to do All-Arms PPS feel awkward wearing the Red Beret, and so want to actually earn the right to put it on their heads. For it is still

the symbol of 'P' Company, a physical representation of all that the Airborne Soldier stands for. When your mind is starting to swim and your knees beginning to go, a mental picture of a Red Beret is far more helpful than is the rather abstract idea of 'passing'. The Red Beret is an actual physical reward to work for. By quietly saying to a man struggling behind the squad: 'Think of that Red Beret', you can bring out his inner reserves of stamina, and breathe new life into him. If he's been wearing the Red Beret for the last six months, however, it doesn't have the same effect.

The Parachute Regiment recruit, though, doesn't have this problem; since not until he has passed 'P' Company does he receive the Red Beret. He has to really want to wear it, and to see the Regimental cap badge above his left eye; he has to really want to be a part of all that those two symbols represent in order to get through the rigours of 'P' Company.

The first hurdle to overcome is the Steeplechase, run on the Friday of Week 12 of recruit training. A 1.3km course run in woods near the barracks, it is the Regiment's version of the Grand National. 'Joe' runs round this twice

'That wasn't so bad, was it?' Sergeant-Major Warner of 'P' Company records the recruits' times after the Steeplechase.

The Milling event during an All-Arms Test Week. One minute's controlled aggression Para-style under the watchful gaze of a PTI from the Army Physical Training Corps.

in his boots, shorts and PT top. It takes an average of 17.5 minutes of determined effort, struggling through water jumps, fighting through mud and clambering over the obstacles scattered along the route.

This grand start to PPS begins with all the recruits lying, on their stomachs, in a line in the middle of the playing fields next to the woods. When a thunder-flash goes off behind them, everyone leaps to their feet and sprints towards the trees and the first obstacle. They've all been over the course before and know that they've got to get to the first water-jump early. Once they have leapt off the scaffolding pole into the putrid water, they are not allowed to get out of the pool via the sides, but have to go up a steep and invariably slippery bank at the front. There are only two routes up this bank, so if 'Joe' doesn't get to the jump quickly enough, he has to hang around on the edge or in the water waiting his turn. And that is the last thing he wants. For the steeplechase is a race against the clock — a test of individual fitness of heart, lungs and legs. And the emphasis is on the individual, of which the Airborne

Soldier is a fiercely competitive example. As he begins to slow down half-way through his second lap, there is nothing that will speed up 'Joe' more than the sound of panting and splashing behind him, and he fights even harder to avoid being overtaken before he reaches a section of the route that is too narrow for him to be passed.

With the Steeplechase over, the recruit — still panting, and covered in mud and decaying leaves from head to foot — returns to barracks to prepare quickly for the next event: the Log Race.

By dropping off the log, he immediately fails 'P' Company

This is a test, not only of fitness, determination and aggression, but also of teamwork. It is designed to find out whether a recruit will 'pull his weight' when the going gets tough, and whether he will push himself to his limits rather than let down his mates. Designed to represent dragging a WOMBAT 120m recoilless anti-tank gun into action, teams of about eight men run around a 2.8km course, carrying a log the size of a telegraph pole. Sections are kept together as much as possible, and besides the 'P' Company staff who assess the recruits,

instructors run with their men to encourage them, trying to ensure that their section wins.

From the moment the teams sprint for their logs and place their hands through the loops of the toggle ropes, to the moment the logs cross the finishing line, is only about 13 minutes, but it seems like forever. For it is 13 minutes of hell. The flat parts of the course are sand, so it's just like running on a beach. As if this were not bad enough, halfway round is what seems to be a near-vertical hill. Struggling up this, 'Joe' really starts to feel the weight of the log. And it's like running on shingle — for every step he takes up, he seems to slip back two. But, though his arm feels that it's being ripped out of its socket and his lungs are gasping for air and his body is begging him to stop, 'Joe' has to keep going. For if he 'drops off' the log, and doesn't get straight back on, 'Joe' lets all his mates down, some of whom he may have spent the last 12 weeks with, since a team that is one man short stands much less chance of winning. Also, by dropping off the log, he immediately fails 'P' Company. And for the student on the All-Arms PPS there is the added incentive that failure means going back and starting the two-week build-up all over again. As one officer puts it: 'If you fall off, that's it; you've wasted six weeks work.'

A man goes down during the Log Race. He must get straight back up, however, otherwise it is the end of his dreams of the Red Beret — this time around anyway.

Once on the flat again, it's back to sand underfoot at the bottom of the hill. Somehow, the sight of the rival log and the finishing line just ahead gets that extra bit out of tired legs and lungs for the final few minutes sprint. Although his team may not have won, Joe has the satisfaction, once he is across the finishing line, of knowing that he's got through the first two events of 'P' Company.

That afternoon comes the 'Milling' — a test, not of fitness, but of courage and aggression. Wearing 16oz gloves, 'Joe' has to stand toe-to-toe with another recruit, and beat the living daylights out of him. The recruits are weighed off beforehand and split into two teams. 'Joe' fights someone his own weight from the other team, so the other guy is also trying to beat the daylights out of 'Joe'. It is not boxing, however; no dodging, weaving or guarding is allowed — it is a test of how much punishment 'Joe' can give and how much he can take, of whether he will keep his head up and press forward, or whether he'll pull back and cower when the fists start flying his way. The recruits who have fought already, or are waiting to fight, sit in their teams around the ring, and every time 'Joe' lands a good punch on his opponent, a mighty cheer goes up from his team; every time his opponent lands one on him, the opposing team roars. And if 'Joe' is forced back by his opponent, then the spectators push him bodily back into the fray. It only lasts a minute, but it seems like the longest minute in the world.

With the Milling over, the recruit is allowed home for the weekend to prepare himself for the coming week of strenuous physical effort. What he needs to do in the last few days before the long endurance tests of 'P' Company is not exercise — if he is not fit enough by now, he never will be — but to eat and sleep. In particular, he needs to build up a stock of carbohydrates in his body to give his muscles the fuel they need to cover the 71km he has ahead of him.

'Would you want the course to be easier? If it was, it wouldn't be worth it'

Monday morning begins with the '10-Miler', a classic Parachute Regiment 'tab'. The DZ (Dropping Zone) where a paratrooper lands is often miles from the objective he has to attack. The '10-Miler' (a 16km speed march), tests the recruit's ability to cover the distance from DZ to objective quickly enough to utilise the 'shock effect' of the Airborne assault. 'Joe' runs this test of fitness and endurance carrying nearly 22kg — his weapon, his fighting order ('webbing'), and his bergen, weighted-down to represent the ammunition he would carry into action. Run as a squad, the '10-miler' is an individual test run in a circuit outside the camp, with the pace set so as to finish in an hour and 45 minutes.

Although it starts off on smooth, metalled roads, it soon starts going cross-country, and before long 'Joe' is scrambling up steep, pebble-covered hills. Past the half-way mark, and 'Joe' is once again running on sand. However, this stretch is also used regularly as a training area for main battle tanks, which leaves the heavy, cloying sand badly pitted and ridged, and therefore not only more tiring, but also more dangerous. But it is not all running. About half is running (known as 'doubling', from 'double quick time'), and half is marching — though performed at such a pace that it is almost as fast as running.

After six miles, 'Joe' is starting to feel the pace. It is getting harder and harder to persuade his body to keep going at the speed he knows it has to. When he is doubling, he can hardly wait for the order to break into quick time — to start marching. He knows that at any moment he is going to hear it, but he must keep pushing his body for that little bit longer until he does; he cannot afford to drop out of the squad. Then at last the order comes. But now 'Joe' finds that he has to really open up his pace, to move his legs quickly and swing his arms in order to maintain momentum. It seems as though quick time is not much

slower than double time. All that seems to change is that it is a different muscle on his leg that he is pushing to the limit. After a few more paces, he cannot wait to hear the order to break into double quick time again.

But, no matter how much it hurts, no matter how much effort it is to keep going, he cannot afford to whinge, even in his mind. Because if he does, he will find himself dropping behind, too far behind to catch up. And it is important to stay with the squad, for, even if he is at the back, it will help to drag him along. Somehow, the squad seems to have an almost magnetic attraction, forcing his body to push that little bit more to stay in there.

All those doing PPS can think back to what the OC 'P' Company said to them on the very first day:

'Would you want the course to be easier? If it was, it wouldn't be worth it. So when you're in pain, enjoy it, and say: "This is keeping the men and the boys separate." And then you know that everybody in 5 Airborne Brigade who has got their wings [for which a volunteer has to pass PPS before he can go on the course] and the Red Beret has actually gone through the same test, and so they are pretty strong characters.'

Also, when Joe is all but ready to 'jack', he has to have confidence in his own strength of character. As one officer on PPS puts it: 'You see other people around you who you know are no better than you. If they haven't quit, why should you?'

When at last he reaches the end of the '10-miler', 'Joe' does not have long to rest, for it is straight on to the 'Trainasium', a confidence course set within the grounds of the Depot. It's aim is to put the recruit under mental pressure, pressure due to height, and to test if 'Joe' has what it takes to jump out of a balloon or an aeroplane. One part of the Trainasium structure is about seven metres above the ground, and 'Joe' has to run along a cat-walk roughly 30cm wide, leap gaps, crawl along two wires about a shoulder-width apart, and other such tests of confidence and nerve. The second part includes the 'high shuffle bars' and the 'standing jump'.

The high shuffle bars are two scaffolding poles, set a shoulder-width apart and about 15m above the ground. With nothing to hang onto, 'Joe' places his heels on the inner side of the poles, the balls of his feet on top, and sticks his arms straight out to the sides. He then shuffles the four metres to the end of the poles, lifting his feet over the scaffolding brackets half-way along as he goes. Just before he reaches the end, an instructor on the ground orders him to stop, bend down, and touch his toes, so he has to see how high up he is. And, although he *is* high, to 'Joe' it seems higher; he seems to be above everything else he can see.

Beneath the high shuffle bars are two platforms. One is about two metres below the poles, and about as wide as the gap between them; 'Joe' can only see it if he looks straight down between his legs. The other is a much larger platform, six metres below the bars, but even this seems decidedly narrow as 'Joe' looks down.

Yet, although the high shuffle bars cause the greatest apprehension for most recruits, it is the standing jump which causes most to fail. 'Joe' climbs onto a platform about four metres above the ground, and when an instructor shouts 'Go!', he has to leap across a gap to another platform, about two and a half metres away. As 'Joe' moves forward to the edge, it seems an impossible distance to cross from a standing jump. But it isn't, as the instructor has proved only minutes beforehand. For the second platform is about a metre below the first, so the recruit's momentum carries him across the gap before he drops into it. This is a test of reaction to orders — of the ability to do what instinct and common sense say you must not do. In this respect, it is the test which most

closely matches parachuting — the experience of throwing yourself into space when the dispatcher shouts 'Go!'

On all the Trainasium tests, 'Joe' is given three chances. The instructor will give the order three times, and if the recruit has still not reacted after the third, he fails 'P' Company, no matter how well he has done on any of the other tests. What it takes to pass the Trainasium is not so much a head for heights, though that makes most of it easier, but the ability to overcome fear. The mental pressure comes because the Trainasium is high enough that if you did fall off, you could break your back. And, when you've watched someone fall off, it rams the message home. If all the obstacles were a metre above the ground, there would be no problem. So, one

Mud is an occupational hazard on the Assault Course. When the instructors cannot read the names emblazoned on the vests, they can read the serial numbers on the helmets.

A recruit takes a downward glance from the Trainasium. This is not a trial of fitness or stamina, but one of nerve. Recruits have fallen from this catwalk — it is 20m high in parts.

way for 'Joe' to overcome his fear is just to keep thinking that it *is* one metre above the ground. In the words of one of the recruits:

'What you've really got to think about when you're up there is that you haven't slogged your guts out for 10 miles this morning and put yourself through pain just to *not* jump over a little gap which you could do on the floor. So really, you've just got to get the momentum and go for it.'

'People do not fight for "Queen and Country", they fight for their mates'

But, even when he has completed the Trainasium tests, the recruit has little time to savour the great sense of relief he feels. Before long, he is back up in the woods where he did the Steeplechase, and back on the Assault Course. Once again, it is an individual effort to test fitness in the heart, lungs, and — most important of all — legs. The course is a 400m circuit with 18 obstacles. 'Joe' has to go round three times — a 1.2km sprint without weight or a weapon.

Few assault courses seem to have such a short gap between obstacles, allowing such little time to recover before aching muscles must push or pull an aching body one more time. By the third lap, only 'guts and drive' can keep 'Joe' going fast enough; that, and the sound of the next person closing up behind him.

After about seven minutes of gate vaults, water jumps and fireman's poles, 'Joe' returns to barracks to prepare for the move back to Wales for phase two of Test Week. This is known as Exercise Steel Bayonet — two and a half days in the Brecon Beacons, with everyone living in the field.

On the first day, 'Joe' has to tab 28km, carrying a weapon, bergen, and all the clothing and rations required for a 48-hour field exercise. A test of endurance rather than speed, the aim is to give the recruit confidence in his ability to cover long distances with a heavy load. That it also tires him out for the tests of the next two days is by the way.

The second day begins with a 15km march over the peaks of Pen-y-Fan and Fan Fawr. At first, the going is fairly easy, up a slope that is not too steep. But it gradually gets worse, changing first to bricks set at all angles, and then just to mud. And the last 500m up to Pen-y-Fan is a one-in-one slope — a real test of determination and drive after six kilometres of almost continuous uphill slog with 22kg on your back. And the final 100m is so steep the recruits are using hand-holds to climb up it.

After going along a ridge, then down into a valley and up again to Fan Fawr, the platoon stops for lunch. But the break is short, and no sooner has 'Joe' sat down, than it's bergens on again for a 10km speed march back to the harbour area, to be completed in an hour and eight minutes.

A would-be Tom attempts the Trainasium's parallel 'shuffle' bars. Shuffling is the easiest way to get along, but small obstacles mean that the feet must be lifted sooner or later.

After a second night in the field, and far from fully rested, the recruits have to face the final test of 'P' Company — the Stretcher Race. This is one of the most difficult events, and not just because it comes at the end of a hard four days. Teams of about 12 men race against each other over 12km of grinding hills. It is designed to simulate carrying a wounded comrade off the battlefield, with four men carrying the specially weighted stretcher while the others take the team's weapons. Every so often, two men on the stretcher change over. Swapping weapons, people, and a moving stretcher takes a good deal of co-ordination and teamwork to get right. For 'Joe', just keeping going is painful. But once on the stretcher, he also gets his share of the pain of 75kg of steel scaffolding and sand channels bouncing up and down on raw shoulders.

For about an hour and 20 minutes, he has to survive it, to give everything for his team to win. If he drops too far behind the stretcher, or refuses to go on it when ordered

A recruit is attended by a medic after being laid low with heat exhaustion on a battle march on the Wales Phase.

The moment that makes it all worth while. Recruits are presented with their Red Berets after passing Test Week.

to change, then he fails. He has let his mates down and they must work that much harder to stay in the race. The CSM of 'P' Company explains why this is so important:

'Basically, people do not fight for "Queen and Country", they fight for their mates. At the end of the day, when we have got a good team spirit going, then because of the responsibility that a man feels for the others on his team, he will not let them down. "P" Company brings that out of them, because no one can hide. It is a course that you can't hide on, and we get the right type of person at the end of it; we get a reliable man on the battlefield.'

If Joe has not let his mates down, if he and the rest of the team have pulled their weight, then his stretcher may still be in with a chance. And if two stretchers are near each other at the end, then there is a final sprint, with cheering and encouragement from the staff running alongside, and the last ounce of strength from 'Joe'.

Across the finishing line, and at last he can rest his aching legs and shoulders and let his body recover. A

mug of warm sweet tea has never tasted so good. Officially, 'Joe' will have to wait to be told if he has passed, but he's got a good idea of how well he's done. For as one of the 'P' Company staff puts it: 'We don't select them, they select themselves'. Although the 'P' Company instructors award points for each event, these are only a guideline. If Joe is ill, but has still worked very hard, he will pass, and the reverse is also true.

The sense of achievement when you know you've got through is second to none. For, as a former OC 'P' Company puts it:

'Anyone who passes this course will have learnt to push himself beyond the normal limits. It is this self knowledge, this confidence that will allow him to keep going when others will stop. So passing "P" Company has a lasting effect on all volunteers, one that will benefit them for the rest of their lives.'

In the final analysis, what is it that makes a man pass or fail? Certainly, one major reason for failing is due to injury — broken feet, sprained ankles, or shin splints gained in training. On the All-Arms course, anyone failing has to start the three weeks all over again, and for the 'crows' it means going back into Falklands Platoon. A warrant officer gives other reasons for a recruit dropping out of Depot:

The Airborne Soldier is fit, but he is no superman. He feels fear, he feels pain

'He has to join for the right reasons, not because he's running away from a girlfriend. "My girlfriend is pregnant", or "I am living with a girl who has three kids" — that ain't no good. Don't come here with problems, 'cos they are going to multiply and you won't make it. That problem will become an excuse to leave when things are tough. There was this bloke who used to look after the whale at Windsor Park, and the whale was ill, and that was his excuse for leaving the Army. It was in all the national newspapers. He shouldn't be in the Army at all.

'A lot of them come here, some for the right reasons — some have had parents in the Army or Regiment before — and some have read too many comics, things like that. And some come here straight out of school, 17 years old, and don't know what they want to do anyway, and it seems like a good idea to go into the Army. Four weeks later, they will come down to earth and know what they are up against.'

But the sort of person who passes is, according to one officer at Depot:

Top: Spare a thought for the unsuccessful. An officer is aided after dropping out of the All-Arms Stretcher Race. Bottom: To the Dakota, and the course photograph.

'The quieter, more self-reliant chap with above average intelligence. He's quick-witted and he's sharp. He may not be academically intellectual, but he's certainly no fool. And it's that sort of character, a well-rounded lad, that makes it. The rather brazen and flashy sort of character — he doesn't make it.

'There is an element of selection by intelligence. We take the top three levels [of the five into which the Army divides potential recruits]. But we do find that, statistically, our passes come from the higher strata of this intelligence rating. The chap right down the bottom end might be very strong physically, but if he is a bit thick, he isn't going to make it. Because it's not just physical. There is a lot more to it — a lot of attitude, and everything else. A lot to learn, and, in my opinion, more for him to learn today than perhaps 20 or 30 years ago, because, technologically, things move along.'

If a recruit doesn't pick up the instruction quickly enough, it's usually because he's not paying attention and concentrating. The staff at Depot are excellent. They are experienced and apply the correct principles and techniques of instruction in a very professional way. And if a recruit doesn't pick it up, then he finds himself getting fitter. For when 'Joe cocks up, Joe gets sweaty', as well as being described as 'pond life' — the ultimate insult to a person's intelligence.

But intelligence is not the main quality required to pass 'P' Company itself. What it needs is motivation and strength of character. The aim of 'P' Company is to select those who have the attributes of an Airborne Soldier; to test for courage, fitness, endurance, determination and controlled aggression. For all but the very lucky, fitness comes through hard work. Endurance can come by switching your mind off from the pain of your body — by concentrating totally on your girlfriend, for example. In the words of one SNCO:

'There are times when you have to put your brain into an alcoholic drink and let it go. When the thing becomes too unbearable, that is what you have to do.'

But courage, determination, and — when the mind can no longer keep out the pain — endurance, are all aspects of controlled aggression. And if that aggression is perfectly controlled, it can be turned on or off at will. It can be directed externally at someone or something else, whenever you want. It can be turned inwards, to get you so angry with yourself that you do what you know you have to do in order to pass 'P' Company; to keep you going when your body is begging you to stop; to force you to jump when your nerves are screaming at you to stand still. For the Airborne Soldier is fit, but he is no superman. He feels fear, he feels pain. But he can force himself to overcome them. It is, in the end, 'all in the mind'.

GREEN ON, GO

After the pain of 'P' Company, RAF Brize Norton might seem like a holiday camp. But the recruit cannot switch off on the basic parachute course. He must take in the instruction and apply it, or he could suffer serious injury. And before every jump, he must overcome his natural fear of throwing himself into thin air.

'It has to be a definite thrust out of that door. You can't just leap out, or you end up on the side of the aircraft with a face full of rivets. You have to punch yourself out through the slipstream, and that takes a lot of aggression. You have all this equipment, and you have been standing with it for ages, so you have to go as quickly as you can. It takes a lot of aggression to throw yourself out.'

As this description by a member of 2 PARA illustrates, it takes considerable physical effort, not to mention effort of will, to get out of a C-130 travelling at speed and only 800ft off the ground. A Para has to really *attack* at the moment of jumping. He needs 100 per cent determination; a half-hearted attempt will not get him through the door. But aggression and will-power are the very qualities that a man will have in abundance if he has passed Pre-Parachute Selection. These are the qualities that 'P' Company looks for; because, when all is said and done, the aim of PPS is to select suitable candidates for parachute training.

Parachuting is, in the first case, what separates The Parachute Regiment from all other infantry regiments in the British Army (except the SAS, and they are a special case). And there is more to this difference than simply the

Men from Pathfinder Platoon, 5 Airborne Brigade free-fall from a Hercules. They use the HALO (High Altitude Low Opening) technique and jump from 18,000 feet on exercises.

TA basic and regular refresher courses being briefed. The PX-5 main chute on their backs is only used for balloon jumps and has a different harness to the PX-4 used from aircraft.

act of jumping out of an aircraft. Parachuting, and everything that goes with it, pervades the whole fabric of the Regiment, producing a set of attitudes quite different to those of any other. These attitudes are in part due to the act of parachuting itself, which bonds man and man, officer and Tom, together as in no other regiment. They are due in part to the training, which is geared specifically towards preparing men for parachuting — in no other regiment must a man pass 'P' Company before he can get in — and they are due in part to the trouble-shooting spearhead role with which the Regiment is charged as a result of being parachute capable.

However, being parachute capable does not mean that the Paras jump into battle as a matter of course. In a peacetime operation, where they were required to rescue United Kingdom citizens caught up in local unrest overseas, for example, the Paras might, strange as it may sound, enter the country aboard civilian airliners and through the civilian airport — if it were still open. And in

the Falklands, they went ashore from landing craft. Parachuting is reserved only for the 'worst case scenario' — for instance, when there is no airfield available, or when the airfield needs to be taken by assault. It is then that the Paras are indispensable; for though it may be argued that other regiments could have coped at Goose Green, and would be well able to handle an evacuation, no other infantry outfit can be sent in when the conventional routes are closed. Parachute capability is, therefore, primarily a contingency; but a necessary one if an army's freedom of action is not to be curtailed.

Military parachute training is the preserve of the Royal Air Force

All this adds up to the fact that while other infantry regiments are busy bulling boots and pressing No 2 dress ready for his pass-out parade, 'Joe' is preparing to embark on a course that will take him one step closer to the dream which kept him going through the past weeks of torment — he is finally going to learn to parachute.

The regular, basic parachuting course (known as Basic Para) is, in fact, the second part of the reward for taking and passing 'P' Company; the first is being granted the right to wear the Red Beret. Basic Para lasts for four weeks and takes place at No 1 Parachute Training School (No 1 PTS), an RAF-run establishment located at RAF Brize Norton in Oxfordshire. Military parachute training in the British Armed Forces has been the preserve of the Royal Air Force ever since its instructors took the very first course, held at Ringway Airport, Manchester, in 1940.

During the Sunday evening before the start of Week 17 of their basic training, those recruits who have convinced the staff of 'P' Company of their potential as paratroopers start to arrive at RAF Brize Norton. They have spent the last three weeks in the Brecon area undergoing Advanced Wales, the bout of live-firing and battlecraft training under field conditions which immediately follows test week. Now, after an all-too-short weekend off, they are returning to military life.

The standard of accommodation is much higher than that on Army camps

As they pass through the gates of what is one of the largest air bases in the country, the Paras first report to the guardroom, from where they are taken across to their barrack rooms. The standard of accommodation on RAF stations is usually much higher than that on Army camps. But not for the Paras the luxury of carpeted rooms; they are consigned to ageing, sub-standard huts for the duration of their stay, and levied a charge against damage into the bargain. Whether this is because of reputation or past experience is not clear!

Work starts the following morning with a session at the Parachute Centre Administration Unit (PCAU). This is the point of liaison between the RAF and Depot PARA on course matters, and is staffed by soldiers of the Parachute Regiment and the WRAC, complete with Red Berets. (This is a sickener for the guys, who have just pushed themselves to their limit, and beyond, in order to earn theirs.) Here the incoming trainees perform the service ritual of completing arrival documentation, including the next-of-kin form, and are issued with the extra kit they will need for the course.

The PJIs are RAF senior NCOs, self-confessed extroverts

Throughout the ensuing four weeks, PCAU remain responsible for the administration of the trainees, and some of the familiar faces of the platoon's Recruit Company instructors from Depot are there to keep an eye on their charges, but the course itself is run by RAF personnel. According to a Para major:

'They are handed over each day to the RAF, ready, at

Practising the PLF — Parachute Landing Fall. With feet and knees together and elbows tucked right in, you can get away with all but the heaviest of landings.

eight o'clock in the morning, and we receive them back at the end of the day's training. We only need half the number of platoon staff. It is really in the hands of the RAF PJIs.'

The PJIs (Parachute Jumping Instructors) are RAF senior NCOs, self-confessed extroverts who have been selected — not necessarily having volunteered for the job — from the service's Physical Training branch. Those at Brize Norton train all the Armed Forces' parachutists. In addition to the Paras, this means the SAS, the para elements of 5 Airborne and 3 Commando Brigades, the RN medics that serve with the Royal Marines, and 2 Squadron RAF Regiment, all of which could have representatives on the same basic jump course as the Paras. They also train the TA Paras, who, with civilian commitments to attend to, have shorter courses and work through the weekends. All this means long hours for the PJIs, as one flight sergeant explains:

'Some of us are teaching the [regular] course all week and work [dispatching] with the TA at weekends. TA, being civvies, only work Friday to Sunday. If they have three Hercules, they need 12 PJIs. There are only five at TA, so they come to me for seven more, first light Saturday morning. Then it's back to work Monday — and that goes on for three or four months.'

All of this adds up to a massive number of parachute jumps. In fact, during 1988 the school conducted a total of 12,570 descents (compared with 8565 carried out by 5 Airborne Brigade), and during the training year 1987-

88, the school's PJIs taught a total of 1375 all ranks.

Trainees on the regular basic parachuting course are introduced to their PJIs after their introductory briefing at the PCAU. For ease of instruction, the course is divided up into 'sticks' of seven or eight men — the trainee Paras being kept together, rather than being dispersed into mixed groups with other-arms personnel. Each stick is allocated its own PJI, who stays with his men for the full four weeks, allowing a rapport and trust to develop between instructor and students.

'They will react to any given situation. When they are told to go, they will go'

The PTS works by its motto of 'Knowledge Dispels Fear', which means that students are not simply told to carry out exercises 'because I tell you to', but have the exercises and the reasoning behind them fully explained before they are called upon to put theory into practice. Similarly, the introduction of each new piece of equipment is accompanied by a lecture on its use and a demonstration of how it works. This is backed up by relentless repetition

A PJI checking a student's PLF position. The recruit has a dummy reserve on his chest. Pulling the red handle on the real thing causes a spring to throw out the reserve 'chute.

of exercises and drills in what is known as the 'command response method of instruction'; that is, by the end of the course, when the trainees are given a particular command they will return the necessary response. As a PJI puts it: 'They will react to any given situation. When they are told to go, they will go.'

The Paras are almost obsessive about maintaining standards

In the experience of the PJIs, the TA Paras, perhaps because they tend to be older, prove more receptive than the regulars, who, after undergoing induction training, Basic Wales, 'P' Company, and Advanced Wales in rapid succession, find taking in even more instruction a little mind-blowing.

However, at least one regular Para has had reason to thank the RAF training system, and the lengths to which the PJIs are prepared to go once they have faith in a particular student's ability to pass. The story concerns a recruit who had a history of being a little unsure of himself throughout his basic training — initially with his

weapon handling and, later, on the 'P' Company Trainasium. The Recruit Company instructors, while noting his uncertainty, were convinced that he was a Para in the making. With extra coaxing and coaching, he overcame his hesitancy with weapons, and eventually passed the Trainasium test and the rest of 'P' Company.

However, with the start of the parachuting course at Brize Norton, all this trainee's confidence problems returned, and the RAF PJIs, always watchful for suspect jumpers, eventually recommended that he be removed from the course. A PJI explains why the RAF sometimes have to take this view:

'You always have to be aware of people's nervous dispositions; aware of people that may be a danger to themselves as well as others, and cannot react quickly to a given situation. There are always a few people during the year that are recalled or taken off the course.'

But the RAF, who know well what a nerve-racking

A student in a flight swing. This is a harness suspended from a frame and is used to practise controlling the canopy during descent — vital in a sky packed with other paratroopers.

Sliding down the outdoor exit trainer. This consists of a 40ft tower with two wires running down from each side. Students slide down the wires suspended in a harness.

experience parachuting is, will insist on an individual's removal only as a last resort. The PJI again:

'You are optimistic, hoping that all eight people in your section will pass, and you coach the weaker ones through, even give them extra tuition in the tea-breaks. You look at people and try to assess them quickly to see how they are picking up on things. But certainly on a basic course, because of the time you have got, there should not be any reason why, if you have someone who is a bit slower or cannot take the information in quickly, there is no reason why they should not pass.'

The Paras were aware of this attitude and, mindful of that particular recruit's record at Aldershot, set about trying to convince the RAF that he was not a lost cause. They cited the soldier's successful struggle to come to terms with himself at Depot, and put up a sufficiently good case for the RAF to grant a reprieve. Extra training at

PTS was suggested and, if that did not work, his removal to Aldershot for intensive attention at the 5 Airborne Brigade RAF detachment — familiarly known as 'Pitts Road' — with the possibility of a return to Brize Norton on the next course.

The more cynical might suggest that the Paras were simply loath to lose the man after spending so much time, effort and money on getting him this far, especially at a time when the battalions are below strength. But that is not how the Regiment works. The Paras are almost obsessive about maintaining standards; it is inconceivable that they would jeopardise future operations by taking on a man in whose abilities and suitability they did not have absolute confidence. Furthermore, selection on merit is central to The Parachute Regiment ethos; it is a principle that is not open to compromise.

In any event, the student stayed, and over the next

Leaving the indoor exit trainer. Commonly known as the 'fan', because of the mechanism used to slow the descent, this is the students' first experience of leaping into thin air.

A look of apprehension on a recruit's face as he prepares to throw himself out of the 'cage' on his first balloon jump. It is a cold-blooded test of a man's ability to overcome fear.

weeks his PJI, helped by Para Recruit Company instructors, worked with him to build up his confidence, using the full range of the various 'Knowledge Dispels Fear' techniques. This included not only spare-time periods of one-to-one tuition, as outlined by the PJI above, but also what one Para officer describes as plenty of 'arm-round-the-shoulder stuff', such as the student's corporal instructor accompanying his charge through specific problem areas in order to provide moral support. In the end, the RAF's methods and the Paras' faith in their man paid off. The decision to keep him on was vindicated, and he now has his wings to prove it. Furthermore, a sojourn at 'Pitts Road' proved unnecessary, and the student passed off with his own platoon.

Although this is perhaps an extreme example of the PTS method of instruction, even at its usual level it is as far away from the parade square as it is possible to get, and it is, after all, a tried and tested method. In the past 10 years, less than nine per cent of regular Paras attending PTS have failed to complete the course — and the majority of these were forced to withdraw because of injury.

The Paras, whatever they might say at other times about the rest of 'Crabair' (the RAF in Army slang), hold the PJIs in high regard, finding them professional and approachable men who inspire trust. Also, they do appreciate the 'Knowledge Dispels Fear' techniques and the importance of having only one instructor. A trainee explains:

'Down at Depot, we had a lot of different instructors, all these different corporals, and you kept on being tested. Here [at Brize Norton] you have one instructor. If you had more than one, you might feel wary. It's different here.'

The first subject on the agenda is how to land correctly

For their part, the PJIs seem to enjoy instructing Army courses, despite the hard work involved. In fact, the flight sergeant is willing to admit that 'I wouldn't swap it for the world, working with the Army — they are a good bunch of guys.'

The introductions over, the first subject on the agenda

Students watching colleagues drop from the balloon tethered at 800ft. This is low enough for those on the ground to see each man exiting the cage.

is how to land correctly. Much attention is paid to mastering this skill, as it could mean the difference between hitting the ground fit to fight, and being a stretcher case with a broken leg before the fighting has even started. To this end, the first period of almost every day of the course is given over to landing practice. And not only landing from the front. The British service parachute (the PX-4) is nonsteerable, so the soldier has no control over the direction of his approach and must be taught how to land backwards and from the side, as well as from the front. In a 40-minute period, each student will perform between 20 and 30 parachute rolls from any angle the instructor cares to name. Landing training is exhaustive — and exhausting. A 3 PARA Tom gives his point of view:

'If you went to watch an exercise, some of the landings are horrendous'

'You get a lot of people come up to you and say, "Oh, we've done parachuting", and all that. Completely different, completely different. You know, we have training, but the civvy can just go to an airfield and do maybe a day of parachuting straight away — plus he has a steerable 'chute. It's totally different; you can't even compare them. Civvy parachuting is a sport. It's easy.'

Having said this, PJIs must on occasion wonder if the long hours spent on landing practice are worth it. The flight sergeant again:

'Well, to a trained trooper, a landing is one that he gets up and walks away from. If you went to watch an airborne exercise, some of the landings are horrendous. But they just get up, shake their heads, get their kit on and get on with the job.'

'You don't want to spend too much time in the air'

The first landing training period is followed by lectures and demonstrations on the three different types of parachute in use in the Forces. The British main 'chute is the PX Mark 4, which is essentially a non-steerable parachute, although it does allow for minor adjustments of position relative to other jumpers to be made on the way down. These are carried out by operating 'lift webs' which, by causing air to escape from one side or the other of the inflated 'chute, allow sideways movement to take place. The PX-4's American counterpart, the T-10, is fully steerable, but this is not necessarily a benefit in a military parachute, and can, indeed, even be a drawback.

One second after exit. The static line attached to the cage has pulled the canopy bag out of the main pack and as the student falls further the rigging lines are deploying.

Four seconds after exit. The rigging lines have fully deployed, pulling the canopy from its bag. Dropping further has caused the parachute to open out. It is now 200ft below the cage.

This is especially the case when parachutists are exiting from both sides of an aircraft — a technique known as simultaneous sticks, or 'sim-sticks'. The problem is that when a steerable parachute deploys, it automatically favours one direction over another, rather than dropping the parachutist virtually directly downwards, as a non-steerable 'chute would. With troops jumping almost simultaneously to both port and starboard sides of an aircraft, this sort of uncontrollable bias could lead to mid-air collisions.

One advantage that the PX-4 certainly does have over the T-10 is the comparative smoothness of descent that it gives because of the way in which it deploys. The US T-10 'chute canopy opens the instant it leaves the parachute

pack, inflating very quickly and delivering a bone-jarring jolt to the paratrooper. In the PX-4, on the other hand, the rigging lines are fully paid out before the canopy fills, relatively slowly, with air, thus giving far less of a braking sensation and a more comfortable ride. A PJI in praise of the PX-4:

'It has a good rate of descent for the job: not too fast, not too slow. You don't want to spend too much time in the air. Safety-wise, it has proved itself over the years to be just a very reliable means of transport.'

'One thousand, two thousand, three thousand, check canopy!'

In contrast with the early days of military parachuting, when Paras went through the door — or even a hole in the floor of the aircraft — with only their main 'chute to rely on, today's Toms carry a reserve: the PR-7. This parachute differs from the main one in two major ways: first, it is worn on the chest; and second, it has to be deployed manually. This latter point may appear confusing on the surface, but it must be remembered that the British forces' basic course teaches the static-line method of parachuting; a method by which the main parachute is opened, not by the Para pulling a 'ripcord', but automati-

A heavily laden officer moves off the DZ after completing his final qualifying jump. Students dread getting injured on the course, as that would mean returning to do it all again.

cally at a predetermined height below the aircraft. In other words, under normal circumstances, the decision on when to open his parachute is out of the Para's hands; only in an emergency, such as when the main fails to open or serious twists occur, is he brought into the decision-making process.

The third parachute that the trainees are introduced to is probably the one in which they will be most interested in the short term. This is the PX-5, which was originally intended as a replacement for the PX-4 but never came into general service because of problems that its pack and the length of its static line caused inside aircraft. The PX-5 is, however, perfectly safe for use from the balloon car, and it is the 'chute that the trainees will wear when they jump from this on the Thursday of Week One.

The day at work finished, the trainees have some time to themselves. Training at PTS is hard and intensive but, outside work, the atmosphere is much more relaxed than at Depot ('It's like a holiday; it's great.') and the facilities, both social and sporting, are impressive, as befits a major RAF station. Most weekday off-duty hours tend to be spent on the camp, both because Brize Norton is comparatively isolated, with only a few pubs within walking distance, and also because the Paras are just too tired after that day's training and too busy preparing for the next to go out for a night on the tiles.

For the first three days, all the training is geared towards the initial descent from the balloon. After that, the students are taught how to exit from an aircraft properly. They are kitted out as they would be for the real thing and taken aboard a realistic mock-up of a Hercules that is fully rigged for parachuting, even to the extent of having the cables for static lines fitted along each side. Here they get their first taste of waiting for the green light to come on, of queueing up and shuffling to the door, of receiving the despatcher's blow which sends them hurtling out into space. They are taught to scream out 'One thousand, two thousand, three thousand, check canopy!', and also put in mind of the fact that this is not just something to shout for the fun of it; if the canopy fails to deploy properly, pulling their reserve is their responsibility alone.

The trainees are given one session exiting from these 'mock doors', as they are known, and then it is on to the Fan Exit Trainer, from which the Paras leap as they would from a real aircraft, but without parachutes, their descent being slowed to a realistic rate by a giant fan. Early on in the first week, this piece of equipment is used purely for exit training, but as the week progresses, it is also used for landing practice and as a means of running through the whole parachuting package, from leaving the aircraft to hitting the ground. In addition, the heights from which landings are attempted gradually increase as the course builds up to the balloon jump. The flight sergeant PJI outlines the sequence from start to finish:

The eerie silence of the balloon cage hanging and swaying in mid-air

'It is all progression from the ground up to 800 or 1000 feet. You start at rock bottom on your landings, then go on to the steps, low ramp, high ramp, wheels, block and tackle, which is where they pull you up. The fan is the next progression. Then you have your tower, then the balloon — it is all a steady progression leading up to the first descent.'

The jump from the 70ft tower takes place on the Wednesday of the first week, and on the same day the trainees get their first-hand introduction to the PX-5 parachute and a balloon-car drill. All week they have been practising Harness Release and Drag (HR&D), which is basically controlling the canopy after the descent, and by Thursday morning they are as ready as they will ever be for the descent itself.

The balloon-car descent has long been invoked by the more unkind of the initiated to haunt the imaginations of 'penguins' (those who have not yet done their jumps course). Almost from the moment they pass through the gates of Depot, recruits are regaled with horror stories of how terrifying the balloon jump is, and it has acquired, along with the 'P' Company Trainasium, the status of a legend in the corridors of Recruit Company. It is generally regarded as being worse than exiting from a low-flying C-130, because of the eerie silence of the balloon cage hanging and swaying in mid-air. There is no engine noise, no wind, no slipstream — just the rocking motion of the cage. The absence of slipstream also means that you feel yourself dropping like a stone, rather than being buffeted by turbulence.

The instructor screams 'Go!', and the trainee is gone, plummeting earthwards

Four trainees at a time accompany their PJI in the balloon cage as it rises to 800ft above the training dropping zone (DZ) at Weston-on-the-Green. Nerves are taut, and it is customary to tell jokes to try to relieve the tension. But some of these trips are silent, because it 'probably makes people as nervous just trying to think up a joke', as one trainee confides.

As the line connecting the cage with the ground tautens, the PJI draws back the bar blocking the exit, and the first candidate steps forward to stand tensely in the door. Once certain that all is in order, the instructor screams 'Go!', and the trainee is gone, plummeting earthwards until, after 200ft, his progress is slowly arrested as the parachute opens. It only remains for him to manoeuvre himself into open space by using the 'chute's limited steering, and to think about the rapidly approaching landing.

Although the balloon descent is not something many want to repeat ('the first one nobody knows what they are doing, the second one you know what you are in for'), some people appear to feel that the stories that surround it are somewhat exaggerated. A trainee who had recently completed his balloon jump had this to say:

'It was all right; not as bad as everyone in the unit said it would be. Everyone says you drop like a stone, and get this big jerk on your back. But in our balloon cage, the lads went up, backed me up, had a bit of a joke on the way up to relieve our nerves. It's really unnerving looking out. I looked over the side and thought, "This is a bit further than I thought it would be". But when it came to going out, it was all right. I was the last man out; all the other lads had gone, and I thought, "I'm not going to let them down and myself down", and it was all right. And as for this big drop — within no time at all the parachute was open. I had a really big smile from one ear to the other, and the feeling of having done something completely different from anything I'd experienced before.'

Nevertheless, refusals do occur, and indeed it has been known for a Para, who for one reason or another could not take the balloon test at the usual time, to go on and quite happily complete actual aircraft descents, and then freeze in the door when asked to jump from the balloon. The flight sergeant PJI describes a refusal first hand:

'I had one on my first ascent. He refused. We did the bizz — got rid of everybody else, brought him down — and he changed his mind. And he was allowed to change his mind, which shook me because I had only just passed [my PJI course] myself. So I was sent up with him on our own, and he frightened me, because he refused again. That opened my eyes. They should never ever be given a second chance; they aren't these days, that was years back. He was petrified, but determined to give it another go, and he managed to convince the officer. I had to stay on it, get up there and throw him out. Of course, I got him on the door, and he froze. I couldn't get him off the door for half a minute. He froze; he was stood at the door there, and he wouldn't budge. God, you know: "I'm not going" — he just couldn't move. Eventually, we were in the back of the cage, we put the bar up and shouted "Close doors" — and he was on his bike. It should never have happened, and it doesn't happen anymore.'

'There is no stewardess service, they can't buy a gin and tonic and duty frees'

These days, anyone who does refuse 'is off this station within six hours, because it spreads like wildfire'. The removal is done quietly with the minimum of fuss, and the man who refused is not allowed any contact with his former colleagues for fear of what effect he may have on their performance over the rest of the course. But in any case, refusals are a rare occurrence; at the time of writing there had not been a single instance for two years, which is a tribute to the 'P' Company selection process.

For those who successfully negotiate their first descent, the programme goes on uninterrupted with more aircraft exit practice. The balloon descent over, the trainees say goodbye to the PX-5 parachute, and Thursday afternoon is spent being introduced in detail to the workings of the PX-4 — the operational 'chute. Week One comes to a close with an in-depth examination of the PR-7 reserve between the never-ending sessions of landings and exits.

All attention is now focused on the C-130 Hercules, and the eight parachute jumps proper that the trainees must carry out to qualify for their wings and full Para status. (This is three more than their German and Israeli counterparts, while the French Foreign Legion demand

Tightening the straps of a container before a jump with equipment at Brize. When a student parachutes with his unit, his container will be bigger, heavier and harder to pack.

six.) A slide show and lecture on aircraft drills takes up Monday afternoon of the second week, and: 'After the slide film there are questions from the lecturer, answers from the students, so they know there is an understanding.' Aircraft drill, both standard and emergency, continues through Tuesday, and then the students are taken up in a C-130 for the air experience flight, which is simply to acquaint them with the aircraft and what they should expect. The flight sergeant PJI explains why this is necessary:

'A lot of people will have flown in an aircraft, but not a Hercules, and we have to take them up and show them there is no stewardess service, they can't buy a gin and tonic and duty frees, and each one is given a chance to stand in the door.'

Wednesday brings the Paras' first encounter with the Outdoor Exit Trainer. Nicknamed the 'Knacker Cracker', this 40ft tower is designed to simulate, with as much realism as possible, what it is like to exit into the slipstream of an aircraft. Cables running from the port and starboard exit points at the top of the tower form a kind of aerial runway down which the Para, 'chuted-up and harnessed in, slides after hurling himself through the door. This is the closest the trainee will get to the sensations of an aircraft descent, and the gentle trajectory provided by the anchored cables aims to replicate the real thing, as described here by a soldier of 3 PARA:

'As soon as you get through the door, the wind takes you — it whips you away. You come out the door, and it takes you right down. Like going down a soft slide almost; that is how I would describe it. They do this thing in training — the Knacker Cracker as we call it.— and you are bounced on wires for about 100m. And that is really an idea of what parachuting is like, but you don't bounce so much.'

'When he says "Come forward", you just wank it all up and go'

The Outdoor Exit Trainer is also used to instruct and test the students on what to do should they find themselves landing in water — how to control their entry into the water and how to jettison the 'chute. The Knacker Cracker is, in fact, the last step in the progression to the aircraft descent, and so, by halfway through the second week of training, the landing part of the course is com-

Students with containerised bergens board the coach which will take them out to the aircraft. The green tube on each container holds the paratrooper's weapon.

The flight deck of a C-130 Hercules from 47 Squadron RAF during low-level manouveres on a tactical approach to the DZ for a training 'operational' jump.

plete, aircraft and exit drills should be up to scratch, and it is time to put it all to the test.

Exactly a week after they drifted to 800ft in the balloon cage, the trainees find themselves sitting in the fuselage of a C-130 Hercules — and this time it is no mock-up; the second Thursday of 'Basic Para' is the day of the first 'clean fatigue' jump from 1000ft. 'Clean fatigue' means without equipment, and with just the main and reserve parachutes strapped to the recruits. The absence of containers and weapons makes the aircraft less cluttered, and allows the Paras more freedom of movement as they make their way towards the door. The routine is exactly the same as it has been in all the practice rounds: Approaching the DZ, stand up and hook up your static line to the rail running along the side of the fuselage; Red on, the first man stands in the door; Green on, go! A novice Para gives his verdict on the first jump:

'Brilliant, unbelievable. Until the 'chute opens, just falling is great. You keep your head back and look up, and you don't actually notice things, just your 'chute opening above you...I just looked over the edge. You

have to go. When he says "Come forward", you just wank it all up and go. Great fun, specially when the 'chute opens and you are just floating there.'

Once through the slipstream and with the canopy open, the Para's attention is naturally drawn to the coming landing. An experienced parachutist with 3 PARA relates what goes through his mind as he descends:

Everything the trainees have learned up to now is gone over again

'You get apprehensive when you are actually going to hit the deck, especially if you are travelling at a fair rate of knots. Then the sheer anticipation makes your body go stiff. You can see the ground coming towards you and you are thinking "I am going to come in heavy", or you know you are going to land really light. Certainly, when I know I am going to come in fairly heavy, the natural reaction is to pull your body up, but you are taught completely not to do it, you know, just wait for it, like. But you can't do that, because anticipation says, "Oh, Christ. Here we go." '

The first descent is done in single sticks, with six men leaving the aircraft each time it passes over the DZ. But the second and third 'clean fatigue' jumps, which take place during Week Three, are more complicated. The second is a 'sim-stick' descent, with Paras leaving from both sides of the aircraft almost simultaneously, and the third is single stick but in larger numbers, which gives the Paras an insight into what a mass operational jump might be like. The form for these two descents has to be learned before the first aircraft jump is attempted because, from Thursday afternoon onwards, training is dedicated to jumping with equipment. For it is jumping from an aircraft carrying over 100lbs of weapons and kit which truly separates the paratrooper from the sports parachutist.

Everything that the trainees have learned up to now is gone over again, this time carrying an SA 80 rifle and a bergen — known in this instance as a Para's 'container' — which is packed with a soldier's essentials. Fitness and stamina are pushed to the limit as the trainees practise landings and exits encumbered by all this extra weight and bulk.

Flying with all this equipment around is an uncomfortable business. Trainees get to experience the cramped aircraft conditions and learn the art of exiting with equipment aboard the mock-up C-130. With the parachute taking up the space on the soldier's back, the container is attached to hooks beneath his reserve 'chute so that it covers the tops of his legs. When the command to stand

up is received, the Paras have to struggle to their feet, some of them carrying so much they need to be helped up, and remain upright bearing all this weight for as much as 20 minutes. After all this, going through the door comes as a relief, but because of the loads they are dragging with them, even this act can be supremely difficult, as the flight sergeant explains:

'We have to physically knock his arm down and heave him out of the doorway'

'On a major exercise, if you have got blokes with 100lbs of kit, you have 300-plus pounds hanging onto that strop, and when he turns into the door, he can't let go of it. You probably think it is easy for him just to slide his hand off, but he is relying on that strop to hold him up, and so we have to physically knock his arm down and heave him out of the doorway.'

The same technique applies if the despatchers get a refusal to jump, which they do occasionally, even from seasoned Paras. The prospect of jumping into space can

Meanwhile, the other students on board grab what rest they can. They will find the aircraft far more crowded at their units, as a C-130 Mk3 can take up to 90 paratroopers.

do funny things to the mind. The flight sergeant again:

'A bloke got wedged on the step with his weapon. Two blokes went past him and out the door, the despatcher got hold of the weapon and heaved him off, but he can't remember a thing about it — mental block. The number of times people have stood in that door for two or three seconds, holding the strop, and you have been trying to bash their arm. And they are so bruised the next day and say, "Well, how did I get that?" They can't remember.'

'The landing is hard on the knees. You get a lot of knees mashed up'

Once they are out the door and have checked that their main canopy has deployed properly, the Paras flick the catches on both the hooks securing the container to their parachute harness. The containers then drop away beneath them on a five-metre-long line. 'No problem releasing the equipment, apart from it crushing your balls when it goes down,' as one trainee confided after his first

Left: With 20 minutes to go, Paras stand up, clip their containers onto the harness just below the reserve, and hook their static lines to wires along the side of the aircraft.
Below: 'Go!' Students shuffle forward to leap out of the doors.

equipment jump. Using this system, the major portion of their kit lands separately. Even so, the first thing that the trainees notice when they try this in training is that their landings are heavier. And the heavier soldiers are affected by this more than the lighter ones, as the 3 PARA Tom explains:

'The parachutes are all a standard size, so if you are big and fat, then you are going to come down, in the Knacker Cracker, a lot heavier. The landing is hard on the knees. You get a lot of knees mashed up.'

But the news is not all bad. The Tom again: 'Jumping with a container is easier. Without it, you are just bounced around and can get twists [in the rigging lines], but with a container, it makes you more stable.'

To start off with, the trainees are issued containers which are already packed, not with kit, but with jerrycans filled with gravel. Before long, however, they need to be introduced to packing their own containers, and this is no easy task, because there is always more to be taken than there seems to be room for. The 3 PARA Tom talks us through what it is like on a jump at Battalion:

'Down at Brize, the containers are already packed, the pre-packed things. Here, you must go through the process — you know, packing your equipment, making sure you have the correct equipment, food and everything. It's mainly space, or rather lack of space. Say you go on exercise for a couple of weeks. You have to account for warm weather, cold, rain — you know, all periods of weather. And ammo, and stuff like that. It's lack of space mainly, but you eventually learn what you need and what you don't, and it is just experience.

'I was more apprehensive of the night jump than of any of the others so far'

'On top of that, you get specialist equipment, and you have to try and pack everything into the smallest amount of space possible. Then you get your support units, like mortars, and they have to jump with base plates, tripods, machine guns — the guns plus all the ammo and specialist sights; they have to be packed and supervised. Some of the containers are hideous, really big, especially for the signals guys and their batteries. It is hard to believe how heavy they are, but it is quite interesting to actually show people, "Look, this is what we actually jump with", and for people to see what you do jump with, because you can't actually visualise the size and weight of these containers. As well as your kit and reserve, you have this container. For the body frame, it is quite a lot of weight to have on yourself.'

For the students training for their first equipment jump, humping these enormous weights is a matter for the future, a reward for passing Basic Para; and they are

now well on the way. By the afternoon of the Wednesday of the third week, all the 'clean fatigue' descents have been completed; all, that is, except for the night jump, and this usually takes place on Wednesday night. A trainee gives his account of jumping into blackness:

'In the aircraft, I was more apprehensive of the night jump than of any of the others so far, including the first one. It was just stepping into the unknown, I suppose. I felt it was a good one as soon as I came out, and I can remember myself saying "One thousand, two thousand, three thousand, check canopy", and I was watching the canopy deploy in the light on the plane. I could see my canopy deploy really clearly, because as soon as the

PJIs about to despatch the first man. This is the worst position to be in as it can mean several minutes braced in the doorway, staring at the ground a few hundred feet below.

A student just after landing on the DZ at Weston-on-the-Green. The yellow strap which connects the rope from the container to the harness is visible beneath his right elbow.

plane disappeared, it was a black circle above me. I looked around and saw the ground as clear as anything and the canopies either side of me. Both were well away, so I steered a way through the middle and got close to the ground, looked down and saw a huge dark circle underneath me. Thought: "Oh, my God, there's someone underneath me", and in fact it was the pit. I then realised...well, first of all a bit of relief, thinking: "Great, it's not a parachutist underneath me, it's the pit." Then: "Oh, my God, it's the pit, it's full of stones and hard bits." Then I looked down again, assessed my drift, and it all worked just like the textbook really...

'I saw myself, I was going straight forward towards these lights. Then the instructor on the ground said there was no wind, so I thought, "Well, I'll let up then." Let up and got tight and just got to the top of the mist, and then got tighter through the mist, and landed. Had the cameras been there, I might even have attempted a stand-up landing; it was really a gentle landing. Then, my first impression on landing was, "My God, the ground's wet." it was quite misty, actually.

'So the parachute's collapsed all round you and you've got to try and find the tie to wrap it up. That was the only difficulty the whole time; took me ages...I had rigging lines all around my reserve and so on, so the HR&D was not kicked into touch, but it was modified a bit when I was trying to uncurl myself from all these rigging lines. They don't teach you that one; it's all teaching you to stop the canopy dragging along the ground, and not what happens if it falls on your head and there's no wind at all.' Paradoxically, jumping in the dark produces a lower casualty rate than dropping in broad daylight. The flight sergeant again:

'You get less injuries on a night descent because you hold your position, or you should do, and you wait for the ground to hit *you*, because you can't see it. On a day descent, you feel for the ground, and that is when you get your injuries — you see the ground rush.'

A trainee echoed the flight sergeant's opinion: 'I just hit the ground like a bag of shit.'

With the night descent out of the way, the students can now concentrate fully on the coming equipment jumps. The first of these is timetabled for the Friday after the night descent but, as with all parachuting, this jump is highly dependent on the weather, and untoward winds can cause it to be postponed. Hanging around plays havoc with the nerves, and the longer the delay, the worse the apprehension. And naturally, a good deal of apprehension accompanies a parachute jump. According to one trainee, who was not alone in his feelings, 'Every jump is a new jump. It is not like you can go up and do the same thing. It gets harder and harder; you can't relax.' This is hardly surprising as parachuting, despite the relatively few serious accidents that occur, is a dangerous activity. Broken ankles or damaged knees on landing are fairly common but, every now and then, a really nasty incident *does* take place. A soldier in 3 PARA describes one such accident:

'The other day we had two bad casualties when we jumped, because jumping on an airfield you have to be *that* quick, and we were so close in the air, and then you get what is known as an air steal, which means that if somebody is below you, then you lose your air. Your 'chute collapses and you have two guys on top of each other. What happened was, they got an entanglement.

They came out, one guy was in a twist, he got caught up in the other guy's rigging lines, and had air steal all the way down. Then at 100ft one guy grabbed the other lad's 'chute, and then his 'chute lost its air for some reason or other — we don't know why — and they both went in from 100ft. You can't use your reserve at 100ft; all that would happen is the reserve would come up in your face and be entangled in your rigging and make the problem even worse. But you have to accept these things. It is the worst one we have had. Yes, we get broken legs and things like that, but...There were broken pelvises...and they had not only broken their pelvises, it was their backs, their heads, and everything else.'

A military free-fall parachutist. The recruit does not do any free-fall on his basic parachuting course. Ater several years in the Regiment he may volunteer for 5 Airborne Brigade Pathfinder Platoon and, if selected, will do an 8-week military free-fall course which is held in the UK and the USA.

Just how much stress there is is illustrated by this trainee's account of a drop that was cancelled after the course was airborne and the doors had been opened: 'The relief. There was no talking on the way up. Once the drop had been cancelled, everyone started talking. You can see the relief.'

Postponements also mean that as many jumps as possible have to be fitted into a short space of time. As a trainee on one particular course relates: 'It took us three weeks to do the first four jumps. It's now going to take us three days to do the last four.'

Obviously, attempting so many jumps in such a limited time is tiring, but the RAF instructors are fully aware of this, and of how the men in their keeping are performing. Any signs of undue strain, and trainees are grounded.

The first descent with equipment is in single sticks from 1000ft; that is, it follows exactly the same pattern as the first 'clean fatigue' descent, which now seems almost like ancient history. The complexity of the pattern increases with the second jump, which is in sim sticks of 10 men, and for the third equipment descent, which qualifies the Paras to wear their wings, 12-man sticks are dropped simultaneously from both the port and starboard sides of the aircraft at 800ft over the Weston-on-the-Green DZ.

'Your eyes are locked on the light, and you go, and nobody can stop you'

This jump successfully negotiated, the trainees are no longer 'penguins', but fully qualified Paras. Yet the course is not over yet; there is still the operational descent to make — with live loads. Thursday morning of the fourth week is spent in preparation, going through operational aircraft drill and then making sure that everything is in its correct place on the aircraft. In the afternoon, the course emplanes for the DZ.

It is during this descent that the newly qualified Paras come the closest so far to experiencing what actually happens on an airdrop. As the aircraft approaches the DZ, chaos reigns aboard as everyone struggles with their kit in the confined space. The operational jump removes any last vestiges of glamour from jumping into battle from the air, especially when the aircraft goes into low-level manoeuvres coming up to the target. The flight sergeant PJI describes the scene, and he is talking about veterans, not trainees:

'Our job has finished once those lads get out there — they then have to start their job of work. And sometimes I

Having checked that his canopy has deployed properly, a paratrooper has unclipped his container from his parachute harness and is now adopting the correct landing position — feet and knees together and elbows tucked right in.

feel so sorry for the blokes doing two hours low level and throwing up everywhere, and they always seem to. If we start getting them ready 40 minutes out, at 20 minutes, when they are due to stand up, that is when it all starts: coming to the objective, ducking and weaving, that's when it all starts.' And a Tom from 3 PARA describes first-hand what it is like:

'From the point of the green light going on, you want to go. Your eyes are locked on the light, and you go, and nobody can stop you; and if they did try to stop you, there would be an incident. When you do go, you want to go because you have been stood there, and been frightened — or apprehensive, certainly. After the waiting, you need to go, and there is nothing worse than going along this thing and then: "Stop!" Because, from then on, you either deflate or become aggressive, it is either one way or the other.

'You are really psyched-up. You can sense the atmosphere in the plane'

'You are physically tired after all the effort, waiting and then actually going. Because you have had seven hours before that — all the packing and checking — so you have done a working day already; you haven't done that much *physically*, but your system has been working inside. You are really psyched-up. You can sense the atmosphere in the plane; 90 guys in a Herc with full equipment; it is hard work. There are different characters, of course. Some sit and go to sleep — automatically. As soon as they get on the aircraft, they sit there and *zzzzz*. And then, other people are having a good natter.

'A battalion drop is worst, because the aircraft is packed and you have different people from different jobs and their containers vary from 120lbs to probably about 180lbs, easy. And you have these huge monster things in a really small space and you have guys falling over each other trying to stand up, or whatever. Then you have a despatcher tyring to do his checks and walking all over everybody. Organised chaos — but it works. It's easy parachuting with hardly anyone in the aircraft, no containers and all that, but when it's full it is very hard work.'

For the operational descent, the jump pattern is sim sticks of 15 — or even 20 — men, and the Paras exit from the operational height of 800ft. This really is the final descent of the course, and as they are driven back to Brize Norton, the members of the course know that it only remains to hand back their equipment, undergo the statutory course debrief, and then their wings will be theirs. After the parade the course disperses — but not for long. For all that they have been through, the Para squad has not finished training yet: two hurdles remain — a final exercise and the pass-out parade.

A TOM AT LAST

After passing the rigours of selection, the new Tom joins his chosen family, The Parachute Regiment. In his battalion, the recruit finds a world full of challenge, one in which a hierarchy of experienced NCOs watches his every move. He first has to prove himself as part of an eight-man rifle section, but he soon finds that he can develop more specialised skills.

When 'Joe' marches off the square after his pass-out parade, it is one of the proudest moments of his life. He felt a tremendous sense of achievement when he passed 'P' Company, and also when he got through Basic Para. But now he has finished what he set out to do so many weeks ago, and he starts to feel relief that at last it's all over, as well as satisfaction that he's finally made it. Wearing a Red Beret, and with wings on his arm, he has become a fully fledged member of The Parachute Regiment.

The dramatic effect of fire from an SF (Sustained Fire) machine gun during a nighttime live-firing exercise.

When he goes on well-earned leave, his family will notice a change in him. As one sergeant-major at the Depot describes those recruits who make it to the end: 'When they have finished here — oh yeah, they have certainly changed. They form a bond with the people, and their whole thing is on a different wavelength; their outlook on life is different. They form a new family. Very few will mix much with their old mates back on civvy street, 'cos they are now in a different world. They are received into the Regiment, the battalion; they have cut their family ties to a certain extent and cleared off and left home.'

For 'Joe', his new 'home' is his battalion, which is likely to be based in Montgomery Lines, directly across the road from Depot. Despite its geographical proximity, however, for the soldier fresh out of training it is a world away in terms of atmosphere. But it may not seem so at first. For it has been the policy in the past to remind Toms straight from Depot exactly why they did 'P' Company, and they are faced with having to do BFTs and 10-milers on their very first day in battalion. And a 10-miler is a regular feature of the company training programme. However, in most other ways, the two establishments are very different.

Instead of the continuous turnover of recruits through Depot, with the weaker ones gradually being winnowed out and the injured forced to drop back to Retraining Platoon, the new Tom joins a family of 500 men. And family is the operative word, since many of the men in the battalion will have known each other for six or more years, providing the basis for a very tight-knit community, one that is imbued with a strong sense of belonging, of camaraderie. This is particularly true of the senior NCOs, some of whom may well have served in the same platoons at an earlier stage in their careers.

The new Tom is posted to a section, very different from the squad in which, as a recruit, he passed through Depot. This section is nominally of eight men, but usually less — due to troops being away on courses, or on leave, or just because of a shortage of manpower, the perennial bug-bear of the Army. The new arrival soon discovers that the other members of the section will usually have

Cleaning up the barrack block for the last time before the pass-out parade. A job 'Joe Crow' has done many times before, next time it will be as a Tom in his new battalion.

been in for some time, and the relationship between the corporal commanding it and the rest is more relaxed. After all, his men are no longer 'Crows', and some of them may even have joined the Regiment when he did.

Having been thrown into such a large family with all its long-established groups, the new Tom has to start to make friends and to fit in with the other men in his section, platoon and company. Besides discovering that he has still got much to learn about soldiering, he must also adapt to the different way he is treated at Battalion. The tense atmosphere of Depot, with the pressure to pass 'P' Company and get through the rest of the recruit course, is gone. However, although the atmosphere at Battalion might seem outwardly more relaxed as far as discipline is concerned, it demands greater maturity from the individual soldier, and shifts the emphasis from external discipline to greater self discipline and responsibility.

A company sergeant major from 2 PARA describes this difference in emphasis: 'Coming from the Depot straight to Second Battalion, they wheel in, thinking that so much is expected of them — and it is. And when they look around them they realise that this is *just* like they thought it was going to be. They see people getting on with it, not just hanging around all day and going for NAAFI breaks or what have you. Every day there is something on, like a training programme. Everybody is kept motivated all the time. And they see that and get into the swing straight away — straight from Depot, straight here, straight in.

In the Falklands, the battle for Goose Green was won by section commanders

'So much is expected of them as an individual. At the Depot they might have a senior NCO or section commander, a corporal, walking around and saying "Look, you haven't got *this* done properly, you haven't got *that* done properly"; but not here. They are here, they have arrived, it is expected of them. If they don't come up with the goods, they are hauled in front of me, and until it's sorted out they continue all the way up the chain, right up to the big boss man himself if necessary. And so the standards of the guys are high, and if they are not then they are quickly found out, and sorted out.'

One of the first to see and sort out those problems is the section commander. In wartime, the section commander has one of the most crucially important posts in the Army. It is said that only two ranks in any army actually give orders: the general, and the section commander — all the others in between merely pass them on. There is a fair degree of truth in that, since it is the corporal in charge of a section who actually has to make the new Tom straight out of Depot do the job he's supposed to do — he has to 'grip' him. He is the man who will lead the

A proud recruit 'bulls' his ammunition boots just before the pass-out parade. He is using a wet piece of cotton wool to apply a very thin layer of polish.

young soldier into battle if the battalion is ever sent into action and, by his character and example, make a scared 19-year-old risk his life to achieve the mission. And it his ability to do that, his ability to mould an efficient fighting team out of his section, that is a major factor in a battle.

In the Falklands, the battle for Goose Green was won by section commanders, through their skill and leadership, 'taking out' trench after trench with their sections. A section commander from 2 PARA describes his role in the Falklands: 'The section commander's basic job is to stay slightly to the rear and always be in visual contact with

the men, because it is very important, especially for young lads — with the adrenalin going and obviously scared — to be able to see you. They need to see an authoritative figure, to be able to look round and know that he is there. Because if they can't — say you are trying to push men out further to the left or right — if they can't see you, because they have gone over the brow of the hill or whatever, they would be worried because they have lost sight of you.

'It is the section commander's job to go round and get the people back up again and moving. One young lad I had kept on looking round to see if I was there and, once he got down, he didn't want to get up again. He was sort of — I had to almost kick him to get him up. But I gave him a short word instead; that is what he wanted. If I had kicked him it wouldn't have done any good. A quiet, friendly word helps them no end.'

When in action, the section commander has not only to think about whether the new Tom is doing his job properly, but he has also to do his own job — one of the hardest in the Army. Simultaneously, he must keep his section on the route given to him by his platoon commander, work out where enemy fire might come from and decide where his section can take cover, decide where he personally will take cover if he comes under fire, pick easily recognisable features to use for reference so that he can tell the section where to fire, and let the

The CSM of Recruit Company on a final inspection before the parade. The staff wear the red and blue lanyard of Depot, while each recruit wears that of his future battalion.

section know what those features are. He must also ensure that his section is not too bunched up, nor too spread out, that it is staying in the correct formation and that every man in his section is alert and observing properly. And while all this is going on, he has to listen in on his radio for his platoon commander to give him further orders or request a SITREP (SITuation REPort), and to hear what the other sections around him are doing.

The section commander is also responsible for the welfare of his men

Within barracks, the section commander is almost the young Tom's teacher, big brother, father and mother all rolled into one. As a junior NCO, he often has to take his section for lessons and revision on a variety of subjects, while on exercises he is responsible for ensuring that his men don't let their standards of soldiering slip. It is his job to ensure that no one in his section falls out of line, and that the discipline within it is maintained. To avoid any potential discipline problems, the section commander will often guide the new Tom, helped out by the more experienced men in the section.

The section commander is also responsible for the welfare of his men, for ensuring that they are fed, watered, and have all the equipment they need. In this he is helped by his section second-in-command, his '2I/C'. Usually a lance corporal (the lowest NCO rank in the Army), it is the 2I/C's job to administer to the needs of the section and so leave the section commander free to think about command — receiving the platoon commander's orders, writing his own, and giving them to his men. Besides administration, the 2I/C also commands half of the section in battle, a 'fire team' comprising three men and himself; the section commander controls the other half, as well as being in overall command of the section.

'If all the administrative side is done, then the section has no problems'

After his section commander and 2I/C, the NCO that a new Tom has most contact with is his platoon sergeant, who runs the administration and discipline of the platoon and platoon headquarters. A company sergeant major from 2 PARA describes the platoon sergeant's tasks in the field:

'The platoon sergeant's role is to ensure that all the administrative work is done so that the three sections in his platoon go rolling on like clockwork onto the next phase and the next phase and the next. If all the administrative side is done, then the section has no problems.

A proud moment as the recruit platoon — much reduced from the 65 hopefuls who formed up on the first day of training — marches onto the square.

'The platoon sergeant has to maintain this administrative side, and ensure that the section commander has no problems within his section — or if he has, to iron them out quickly, to get rid of the problem. It becomes a platoon sergeant's problem to sort out. It is his job to ensure the men have ammunition to carry on their role, to keep the momentum going like clockwork, to ensure that they have rations, to ensure that if one of them is wounded he is got back to the regimental aid post and, if we have prisoners of war, to quickly take them out of the section commander's hands.'

This system works, in parallel to the chain of command, all the way up the structure of the battalion. Within a company (three platoons), the company sergeant major (CSM) and company quartermaster sergeant (CQMS) do the same job for their platoons as the platoon sergeant does for his sections. And, as the combat supplies go down the 'admin chain', so the requests for equipment travel up it, as a sergeant major from 3 PARA describes: 'Any good soldier administers himself. He just has to put in his requirement to the section commander, who puts it in to the platoon sergeant, who sends it to the colour sergeant [CQMS], who then sends the item to the soldier.'

The rewards for hard work over the gruelling weeks of training: the inspecting officer presents awards for best recruit, and the best shots on the SA 80 (both IW and LSW).

But the platoon sergeant's job is not just 'admin'. He is also responsible for discipline within the platoon and for ensuring that every one of its members maintains a high standard of basic soldiering skills. Together with the platoon commander, the platoon sergeant must also keep up the morale of the men. All these aspects of his job are very much interlinked, and how well he deals with them is determined by one thing and one thing only — his ability to lead. A senior NCO who was a platoon sergeant with 3 PARA in the Falklands describes what it was like for him on top of Mount Longdon under intermittent artillery and mortar fire for 30 hours:

'Well, I have always taken the attitude that, provided you get round amongst the soldiers and let them see that you are alright — and it's certainly true at platoon sergeant level, where a lot of the younger soldiers look to you as a kind of father figure anyway — if they can see that you are alright and are getting round amongst them, then they will

knuckle down. It is when everybody seems to disappear and nothing seems to be happening, that's when people start to get frightened, because they look for the leadership.'

The platoon sergeant's job is made easier by the standards that the Toms expect from each other. As a sergeant major from 2 PARA put it: 'Amongst themselves they keep their standards high. If one of them is slacking, then the private soldiers, the Toms alongside him, notice first, and then the section 2I/C and the section commander will notice: it needn't get to platoon sergeant level. And it is good, if you can keep and maintain that, which we have.'

Also, a soldier who is unhappy with the Regiment can always ask for a transfer. The sergeant major again: 'Often, if there is a problem at the soldier's level — like wanting a transfer — a man will come up and ask for an interview through his chain of command: platoon commander first, then through to me, the sergeant major, and right up to the company commander. Sometimes he will say he doesn't like it, or he wants to get a trade in this or that. But the system is there so that if he doesn't want to be part of that team — and if *he* doesn't want to be there, *we* don't want him to be there — we will get rid of him and get him to the regiment that he wants to be in. And it is quickly sorted out by his fellow soldiers. If he doesn't like it they will say, "Well, why don't you get yourself an interview?", and at that level it is sorted out. In the pub downtown, at the bar, they will talk about it: "No, I don't want to be number three rifleman of number two section" — "Well, get the hell out and let's get somebody there that does", and that is operating all the time.'

It is often said that sergeants are the backbone of the Army, and it is certainly true that the high quality of the warrant officers and senior NCOs in The Parachute Regiment is one of the major reasons for its excellent standards and record of success. The company sergeant major from 2 PARA again: 'The standard of senior NCOs and warrant officers is higher [than in other regiments], and this proves itself all the time by the course reports that come from the infantry schools.'

And the same company sergeant major from 2 PARA tells just how important it is for the senior NCOs and

Warrant Officers to maintain those standards in the Regiment: 'Everybody has their own job to do, and I can get on with my job, which happens to be making sure that everyone is pulling their weight. But if I am a section commander or platoon sergeant, if I can get on with my job knowing that Private Smith, 100 metres away from me down on the end there, is doing *his* job, and if he is not doing his job then somebody will quickly stamp on him and get him to do his job, then *my* job becomes so much easier. If you can keep everything nice and simple, all the way along the line, it makes life so much easier and missions so much more able to be accomplished.

To become an RSM in the Paras is the ambition of many a young Tom

'So it was very important [in the Falklands] as far as I was concerned, and we have always had that standard and have always maintained that standard and will always demand that standard. Once we start losing that standard, then we have to keep chasing Joe Bloggs down on the corner or 150 metres away, and of course we won't be there to meet this deadline and the next, and so on and

A lance corporal in 2 PARA (shown by the blue DZ flash) changes the magazine on his IW version of the SA 80 in a live firing exercise. The Tom behind is firing the LSW variant.

A Tom must train hard under all conditions. Crawling through sewers is one of the main ways of moving when Fighting In Built-Up Areas (FIBUA).

so forth. That is very important, and so we do demand this standard. Of course, if it is not done, then that man is quickly sorted out and put in the picture and, if he doesn't like it, off he goes.'

But the man ultimately responsible to the commanding officer of the battalion for maintaining the standards within it is the Regimental Sergeant Major — the RSM. Usually, he is only seen by the ordinary Tom when the battalion is gathered together en masse, or when the young soldier is committing some heinous crime — such as eating while walking around barracks. The RSM then has an uncanny knack of appearing from nowhere, heralded by thundering tones of reproach.

To become an RSM in the Paras is the ambition of many a new Tom. But it is a long, hard, and selective process, taking 18 to 20 years and a lot of character and ability.

The first step on the ladder is to become a lance corporal — the hardest rank to gain and the easiest to lose.

For a man is taken from amongst his mates and put in charge of them. He has to learn that he is no longer just 'one of the lads', but that he must get things done, not because he is a friend of the Toms he is in charge of, but because of his character. However, he must not go to the other extreme and let the rank 'go to his head'. That causes tension within the section, destroys team spirit, and could be disastrous.

If a Tom has potential, then he may be pushed forward to do a two-week 'drill and duties' cadre (course) within a year of joining the Regiment, though two or three years is more common. If he does well on that, then he will receive the one stripe that denotes that he is a lance corporal. To become a full corporal takes about another three or four years and a much harder course — the Section Commanders' Battle Course (SCBC). After that, and if he is good enough, he will go on to do the Platoon Sergeants' Battle Course (PSBC).

Both these courses are held at the NCO's Wing of the School of Infantry at Brecon. Brecon was formerly the battle school of The Parachute Regiment, and this tradition lingers on, both in the content of the course and in the proportion of Parachute Regiment instructors and students. The importance that the Regiment places on these two courses helps greatly in maintaining a high standard of NCO, as the Sergeant Major from 2 PARA describes:

'Every corporal is worth his weight in gold, and wants to be a sergeant'

'A corporal in my company would not expect to make sergeant until he had done both Junior Brecon and Senior Brecon [SCBC and PSBC], whereas in an ordinary infantry regiment, just one of the courses will do for becoming a sergeant. Normally, they prefer them to do the platoon sergeant's course, obviously, but in this regiment you don't normally get your 'full screw' [corporal] until you have done Junior Brecon, and you don't get your sergeant until you have done Senior Brecon.'

If he is promoted to sergeant, then the corporal becomes a member of one of the most exclusive clubs in the world — the sergeants' mess — as a company sergeant major from 3 PARA describes:

'Every corporal is worth his weight in gold, and wants to be a sergeant. The sergeants' mess is a club that normally takes about nine years to get into and, once you are there, you are fairly home and dry, although it doesn't mean you can stop working. It is a big plus to get into the sergeants' mess. More work is done there from 10 o'clock on a Monday morning until half past, talking to your own kith and kin if you like, than is actually done in the office. It is a powerhouse where things are actually sorted out.'

After two or three years in a standard rifle company, a Tom may want a change, and choose to transfer to a specialist platoon within the battalion.

The infantry battalion is like the Army in miniature since, unlike a REME workshop or a Gunner regiment, the infantry battalion must be able to fulfil its mission independently of any support. This is particularly true of a parachute battalion, which often has to work on its own, as there are never enough aircraft to get everyone you want onto the ground at once. So, just as the Army as a whole has artillery regiments for indirect fire support, so the infantry battalion has its own 'pocket artillery' — the mortar platoon. While the Army has the Royal Signals, the battalion has the signals platoon, and it even has its own 'Intelligence Corps', in the form of the intelligence section at battalion HQ.

Instruction does not stop when a Para leaves Depot. Though he has learnt a lot during his recruit training, there is still much more to learn when he reaches his battalion.

Each of these platoons and sections has a character all its own, a character different from that of the rifle companies and one that is moulded by the men the unit draws in to perform its specialist task.

Perhaps the most important of these platoons is the signals platoon (although the members of the other specialist platoons would, no doubt, disagree). The signals platoon is responsible for all radio and telephone communications within the battalion — for manning the radios that link the companies to battalion HQ, and for training all the other radio users in the battalion.

This role places a considerable responsibility on the young privates and lance corporals of the platoon. If they fail in their job, the commanding officer (CO) of the battalion cannot receive information or pass orders to his company commanders — in effect, he cannot command the battalion. Because they depend so much on their radio operators, commanders at every level tend to build up a special relationship with their signallers. As the CO's radio operator of 3 PARA in the Falklands puts it:

Recce platoon is the battalion's eyes and ears

'Signaller and company commander are usually pretty close. It is a very important relationship really, because *you* are looking after *him* in a way; you are telling him what the score is and so on. You are there as a sort of moral support, I suppose. You have your own little team there and it gives him a feeling of confidence. [The CO's] signal detachment had just changed before the Falklands and he went mad and said, "I want the same lads". It was quite an important relationship; we were the CO's crew, and proud of it.'

But the signaller's responsibility extends beyond keeping the CO informed. He carries the most powerful weapon in the company — with the radio on his back he can call down mortar and artillery fire, even request an air strike. And the lives of the rest of the battalion depend on him, for he is the only soldier who speaks to the enemy.

Every radio transmission involves three people — one sending, one receiving and one, the enemy, eavesdropping. One momentary lapse of concentration and the signaller can give away vital information. A transmission just a second too long allows enemy direction-finding equipment to bring artillery fire onto the signaller and his HQ. It is a very heavy responsibility to thrust onto the shoulders of a young private or lance corporal.

One of the most important aspects of training is the 'live-firing attack'. Here, troops move down-range while firing live rounds at wooden targets in order to test their weapon handling and shooting skills.

While the signal platoon believes it has the most responsibility — and the most brains — the reconnaissance platoon *knows* it has the best soldiers. Certainly, in the battalion military skills competition, recce platoon is the one to beat. Usually working in four-man patrols, the platoon is the battalion's eyes and ears. In defence, the patrols sit well forward of the main battalion positions and report back on enemy movements. Before an attack, they come directly under the command of the CO who, along with the IO (Intelligence Officer), decides what he needs to know about the enemy or the ground ahead, and tasks the patrols accordingly.

As recce operates totally independently, not working alongside the rifle companies as do the other specialists in the battalion, the members of the platoon tend to be even more individual than most Paras, and even more self-sufficient. And recce platoon rarely has problems filling places, for there are always a number of men from rifle companies attracted by the challenge of long patrols, the rigours of staying hidden in a hole in the ground for days on end, and the camaraderie of working in small groups.

The sniper section works very closely with recce platoon, and is in many ways similar. As with members of recce, snipers must also be able to remain undetected for long periods, waiting for an appropriate target to present itself. They are, of course, good shots, but the ability to shoot well and accurately can be taught to most people. What is far more difficult to teach a man is the ability to blend in totally with his surroundings — which is the real hallmark of a good sniper.

The emphasis is on slick drills without the slightest mistake

The sniper section attached to 3 Para received the new L96 sniper rifle only just before they participated in the 1988 United Kingdom Land Forces Sniper Concentration, and in consequence had very little opportunity to familiarise themselves with the new weapons. Even so, they still managed to go on to take both first and second place and win the competition. Perhaps it is something intrinsic to Parachute Regiment training, its emphasis on good camouflage and concealment during training in Wales, or its basic professionalism, that gave the snipers from 3 PARA the edge.

Like the recce platoon, the snipers rarely have problems finding volunteers for their specialist role. But any would-be sniper must first go on a course at Warminster, a course with only a 45 per cent pass rate. So, although volunteers may be numerous, those who finally become members of the sniper section are much fewer.

Totally different from the sniper section and recce platoon is the mortar platoon. Rather than 'sneaking about

Men wishing to join 5 Airborne Brigade's Pathfinder Platoon undergoing selection at Okehampton in Devon. Most of the men in the platoon come from The Parachute Regiment.

with grass tucked in the top of their boots', as some Paras irreverently describe the activities of recce, in a good mortar team the emphasis is on slick drills without the slightest mistake. If they set the wrong elevation on the mortar, or load a bomb with the wrong charge on it, then it may well be the rifle companies rather than the enemy that are bombarded with high explosive. Yet the mortars must also come into action quickly, to provide the rifle companies with fire support when it is needed — five minutes later may be four-and-a-half minutes too late.

But just setting up the mortar to fire in the right direction is a complex task requiring skill and judgement on the part of the 'Number One' — who also commands the crew, or 'detachment' as it is known. The whole process needs a fair degree of intelligence to understand and a lot of practice to get right. Which is why the mortar platoon considers its job one of the most technical in the battalion.

However, members of the platoon do not just operate 'on the mortar line', as it is called. They are also responsible for calling down the mortar fire and adjusting it onto the target. The men who do this are known as 'Mortar Fire Controllers', or MFCs. They work right forward, so that they can radio the location of targets back to the mortar line and, once the rounds start landing, radio back the corrections necessary to hit the target.

Understanding how the sophisticated MILAN works requires intelligence

An indication of the high level of individual skill and responsibility demanded of all ranks in any infantry battalion, whether or not it's from The Parachute Regiment, is that the job of the MFCs is carried out by sergeants attached to each rifle company, while in artillery regiments the same job is entrusted to captains and WO1s.

Mortars have the same problem as the signals platoon as far as recruiting is concerned, for the Toms in the rifle platoons see signallers and mortarmen straining under

very heavy loads and think themselves lucky that they are not carrying such weight. In other regiments, the mortars are transported in Land Rovers. Because there are never enough aircraft to drop sufficient vehicles for the battalion, the platoon often has to man-pack its mortars, each member of a detachment carrying a different piece. Jumping with an 11kg baseplate, sighting equipment and mortar bombs in your container is not an enviable task, as this raises its weight to over 60kg.

Another platoon with considerable weight to carry is the anti-tank platoon. Parachute Regiment battalions are unusual in that, not only do they have the MILAN wire-guided anti-tank missile, but they also have WOMBAT — a four-metre long, 120mm-calibre recoilless rifle carried on the back of a Long-Wheelbase Land Rover. WOMBAT is useful, not only for knocking out tanks, but also for blowing holes in buildings with its 12.8kg HESH (High Explosive Squash Head) shell.

The two types of weapon — MILAN and WOMBAT — tend to attract two types of soldier. Understanding how the sophisticated MILAN works requires intelligence,

Selection for the Pathfinders takes place in Wales.or, as here, on Dartmoor. Exercise 'First Try' tests patrolling skills and the ability to carry heavy weights over long distances.

while the quick loading of 27.2kg WOMBAT rounds calls for strength in a man's upper-body. In the days when only WOMBAT was used, the whole of anti-tank platoon rode in Land Rovers along with the guns, so the fittest men entering Support Company would tend to be assigned to the mortars, since they had to 'tab'. Now, with the Number One of a MILAN detachment carrying 47kg, the fittest of the intake go to MILAN.

'The whole area in front of you is just ripped apart before you get there'

Another very fit platoon is the SF, the sustained fire machine gun platoon. Parachute Regiment battalions were the first to be equipped with .5-inch heavy machine guns. Both 2 and 3 PARA learnt the effectiveness of '.5s' in the Falklands, when they were on the receiving end of

Security is always tight at any Parachute Regiment establishment — whether it be Depot or a battalion location. This means doing 'stag' — the bane of any soldier's life.

As a Falklands veteran from a rifle company describes it: 'At night, when the SF are opening up, you just have a sheet of tracer in front of you and it is devastating — the whole area in front of you is just ripped apart before you even get there. But you feel so safe, because you know that nothing is going to come between you and that tracer.'

Often, a Parachute Regiment battalion has to operate without tanks and with only a couple of 105mm guns in direct support, so the firepower of the mortars and SF is far more important to it than to a battle group in Germany, for example, with its tanks and divisional artillery.

A colour sergeant from Depot: 'Being in an SF team is hard work. But clear satisfaction is gained from being part of a small, highly trained team that can work hard, produce the goods, and remain cheerful throughout.'

The ability to supply quickly and efficiently is crucial

For minor engineering tasks, the battalion has its own 'Sappers' — the assault pioneer platoon. This allows specialist, highly-trained Royal Engineer units to get on with brigade tasks rather than travel great distances for simple jobs. As a sapper from 9 Para Sqn Royal Engineers ruefully recounts: 'I have had tasks during my Army career which involved going 30-40km in a vehicle. Then, when I have got there, all they have wanted me to do is lay 10 measly little sandbags.'

Assault pioneers are not only trained to lay those 10 sandbags, but also to lay, detect and lift mines. They also receive training in demolitions, field defences (trenches and barbed wire), watermanship (boat-handling skills) and water supply. The chance to blow things up, and the wide variety of tasks involved, attracts many eager and willing volunteers, so the platoon can usually find men to fill its gaps.

Very different in ethos to the snipers and SF platoon is the MT (Motor Transport) platoon. This is often composed of older soldiers who have served their time in rifle and support companies and who have had enough of 'tabbing around the cuds'. While the platoon may be a little more relaxed than others in the battalion, all its members are still Parachute Regiment soldiers — they have passed 'P' Company and Basic Para. They still retain their infantry skills, but are also good, experienced drivers. Without them, moving supplies, ammunition and men forward is many times more difficult. And in a combat situation, of course, the ability to supply quickly and efficiently is crucial.

The intelligence section does most of its work in battalion HQ. Including the Intelligence Officer (IO), it is five strong, and has some of the most knowledgeable men in the battalion, men who know everything there is

their awesome firepower. Since then, battalions have acquired examples to provide low-level air defence and to beef up the 7.62mm General Purpose Machine Guns in SF platoon.

The SF platoon's job in an attack is to provide a concentration of firepower strong enough to make the enemy keep their heads down, so allowing the rifle companies to assault the objective relatively unharmed (known as 'shooting' the rifle companies onto the objective). In defence, on the other hand, the platoon is usually split between the rifle companies, in order to provide long-range protective firepower.

But the rifle companies do appreciate the SF; not perhaps when they are helping to lug the prodigious amounts of ammo that the guns devour, but certainly when it comes to the actual battle.

to know about the likely enemy, including opposition tactics, vehicles and organisations. They also know about Nuclear, Biological and Chemical (NBC) warfare, and are able to plot and predict the effects of such a strike. A tight-knit group that works closely together, its role is to give the commanding officer every conceivable piece of relevant information about the enemy that it can. Since, in war, the situation can change very rapidly, the Int. Section receives regular 'intelligence summaries' from Brigade headquarters telling of changes to the enemies strengths and dispositions. But the Int. Section is also responsible for co-ordinating intelligence-gathering within the battalion — the Intelligence Officer in particular is involved in the planning and co-ordination of reconnaissance patrols by recce platoon and the rifle companies. Another of their tasks is to debrief prisoners of war.

No source of information can afford to be overlooked, and so the intelligence section needs plenty of ABI (Airborne Initiative) to do its job properly. This was shown by the Int. Section colour sergeant from 2 PARA in the Falklands. After the battle for Goose Green, he simply phoned through to the settlements at Bluff Cove and Fitzroy to find out if there were any Argentinians there.

Until recently, all these platoons recruited their men from the rifle companies, generally taking a soldier with two or three years experience. As we have seen, some of the platoons and sections — such as recce, snipers, and assault pioneers — have no problems with attracting volunteers, because their roles are seen as being exciting or glamorous. For other platoons, though, it can be very different, often because the Toms in the rifle companies do not realise how interesting these other jobs are. As one RSO (Regimental Signals Officer) describes it:

Often, the new subaltern feels he has to justify his orders

'Well, we run a cadre [training course] once a year, and we get one or two volunteers, but not many. People are generally press-ganged into it — they don't get to choose until we have filled the places we need to fill. It is unpopular as far as outsiders are concerned, because of course they see the signalmen trudging round behind the OC with bloody great rigs on their backs.'

But without the signallers with 'bloody great rigs', without the man-packed mortars and the SF, then the job of everyone else in the battalion would be very much more difficult — and that is true for the officers, from the CO down.

For one of the unique aspects of The Parachute Regiment is the relationship between the officers and the Toms. Traditionally in the British Army, this has been *the* great divide, and in many regiments it still is. But not only

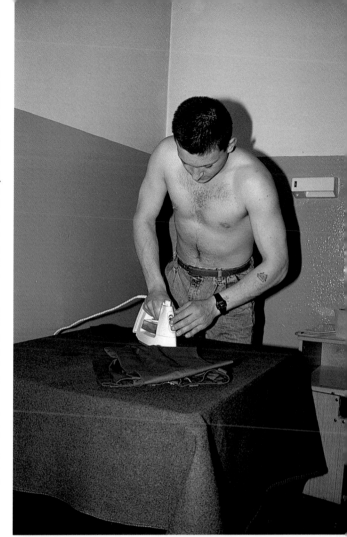

Top: Pressing kit, a memorable feature of Depot, continues at battalion as standards learnt in training must be maintained.
Bottom: A WRAC attached to the Paras for clerical duties.

All Army establishments require back-up personnel to look after the front-line soldiers, and those of The Parachute Regiment are no exception.

with, but he has never had to command them before. And he is in for some surprises.

At Sandhurst, he was taught that when he said 'jump', 30 men would jump; all was 'simple and pre-ordained by military tradition'. His first misconception is shattered when not 30, but only 15 men parade before him. He then discovers how frequently they ask why they are jumping, what the purpose of a particular jump is, or even: 'Why don't we buy a trampoline?' Nothing in his Sandhurst training has prepared him to meet the confidence and intelligence of the Parachute Regiment soldier — how much he thinks and how ready he is to express his opinion within the framework of Army discipline.

Often, the new subaltern is almost tempted into arguments, or feels he has to justify his orders. This is when his platoon sergeant steps in to silence dissenting voices and ensure that the platoon commander's orders are carried out. Before long, though, the young officer is learning to stand on his own two feet; to forestall questions and comments by clear orders and a firm stance. But he is still learning from his platoon sergeant. A sergeant major from 2 PARA explains:

A friendship born out of mutual respect and working together

'Young officers coming into the Regiment need educating by a good platoon sergeant. A young second lieutenant coming into A Company, which is a rifle company, all of a sudden he is in charge of 20-odd men, and he has a 27-year-old platoon sergeant who has 10 or 11 years overall military experience. It is quite a step for that officer. So, the platoon sergeant takes him and teaches him. Now, there is a way of teaching officers and a way of teaching ordinary men. The officer isn't *told* what to do, he is *guided*, because he is obviously not expected to know everything there is to know about morale, etc. When he first arrives, he has read about it and been taught about it — but he hasn't used his training practically. This is the first time.'

The platoon commander, however, is still in charge of his platoon, as another company sergeant major describes it: 'Well, you have to remember that for the platoon commander, it is *his* platoon, so *he* makes the decisions on everything that happens. Initially, the system in the Regiment has always been that the platoon sergeant looks after his platoon commander. He advises him very strongly, right from the moment the chap actually arrives. And it is only after about a year or so that the platoon comman-

does The Parachute Regiment contain a high proportionm of officers who have come up through the ranks, it also contains many officers whose performance during recruit training led them to be sent to Sandhurst for officer training. They are, therefore, officers who wanted to be members of The Parachute Regiment before they wanted to be officers.

The attitude of the officers towards their men is, therefore, quite unusual for the Army. But it is one that has to be learnt by the brand new officer straight from 'The Factory' (Sandhurst). To him, the battalion seems even stranger than it does to the brand new Tom. The young subaltern is 'super-keen', and can't wait to make his platoon the best in the battalion. But there is one factor missing from his appreciation. He has been told about 'the men', the 'other ranks', the soldiers he will have to deal

Sport is an important part of life both at Depot and in the battalions. It promotes team spirit, co-ordination, and is a very good way of maintaining fitness.

A fire team from 2 PARA go into all-round defence. An Airborne force is most vulnerable in the first few minutes after it has landed, so rallying drills must be very slick.

der has the experience to actually run a platoon as well as the platoon sergeant can. So, if you like, it is a gradual crossing over of power, and eventually, when a good platoon is running well, the platoon commander is making the decisions and the sergeant is just concentrating on the administration and discipline of the men.'

For this change-over to occur smoothly, the platoon sergeant must respect the young subaltern. The sergeant major from 2 PARA again: 'The platoon sergeant and platoon commander should get on fine, and if they do, then you have the basis of a very good platoon. If there is a personality clash between the two, then it can be a problem. But it is not one that can't be overcome; we can always move people around. A problem like that is quite rare anyway, and the reason it is rare is because the officer knows what to expect from a platoon sergeant, and the sergeant knows what is expected from the officer.' However, if the two men *don't* get on, then the first people who suffer are the Toms.

The relationship between the platoon commander and his sergeant should be a close one, a friendship born out of mutual respect and working together. Both men should keep each other well-informed, and there should be no 'hiding' facts from each other. Just as a platoon sergeant educates a young subaltern, so an experienced officer will guide a brand new platoon sergeant.

In time, a bond develops between platoon commander and platoon sergeant. They 'watch each others backs', covering for one another and helping each other out. And if something goes wrong in the platoon, then the platoon commander is dragged before his company commander for an 'interview without coffee', and the platoon sergeant is taken to task by the company sergeant major for the same mistake. This facing of adversity together helps bind sergeant and subaltern still closer.

'We have been through some bloody tough times together'

Similarly, sharing responsibility develops a loyalty between the two men. The company sergeant major from 2 PARA again: 'The relationship can form the basis of a very good bond between the platoon sergeant and the platoon commander so that, later on in life — and especially in this regiment — you see this young platoon commander end up as a company commander with that young platoon sergeant as his company sergeant major. And that is great, isn't it?

'Company commanders and company sergeant majors say: "Our bond has worked; we have done it and got there and we've done OK." We have got some very good lads, and we have been through some bloody tough times together, and I can say to my platoon sergeant: "Watch over him [a new subaltern]; this is how *you* should do it, tell him how *he* should do it". And so on.'

In The Parachute Regiment, this bond is much easier to build up because of the relationship which exists between officers and men. It is far closer than in most other British Army units, and there is certainly not the distance between officers and other ranks that there is in units like the Guards, for instance. A company commander from 3 PARA describes the relationship:

'It was brought out in the Falklands, I think. You go with what you've got, and the men you go with are in

exactly the same position as yourself, and you have to muck in, digging your bit of the trench. You live and eat and fight together. I think the men expect you to do the same things that they have to do, and that is the ethos of The Parachute Regiment, if you like — we are all measured against a common standard.'

The mutual respect born in the trials and tribulations of 'P' Company

And that common standard is 'P' Company. A company sergeant major from 2 PARA elaborates: 'With all the young officers and men in the Regiment, it is a good thing. They do rely a lot on each other, and the bond comes from the fact that they all know that the officer, like the enlisted man, has had to come through "P" Company, and that bonds us, because it is very difficult. I can look at any officer in the Regiment and know that yes, he has come up to that grade, he has done the same as what I have done.'

That mutual respect born in the trials and tribulations of 'P' Company also affects the Toms' views of officers

The LSW variant of the SA 80. With its x4 magnification SUSAT sight, high-velocity SAA 80 round, and bipod, it is even more accurate than the IW version.

from other regiments who have not done 'P' Company. The company sergeant major again:

'If we have an officer from another regiment attached to us, then straight away he has to earn the respect of the men, because he hasn't done "P" Company. Whether you like it or not, that is a fact. On the other hand, if he has done "P" Company and has wings on his arm, then he knows straight away that he hasn't got to earn their respect, that the men will already respect him because of that bond, and therefore it is much easier.'

Besides 'P' Company, parachuting itself helps to bond officers and men together, as a staff officer from 5 Airborne Brigade describes: 'One thing you can say about it is that parachute training is a great leveller. The Brigade is a great family, and one has no problems just going up to a bunch of parachute soldiers and engaging them in conversation and finding out what is going on. There is a great tendency, once you come back here as a field officer, to walk around and bump into people who are now sergeant majors and those sort of types, people that you knew when you were a subaltern and they were corporals, and you know that there is a great deal of camaraderie there.'

Standing next to one another in the aircraft before a drop may be the commanding officer and the newest Tom, but they must still check each others 'chutes and harnesses and stand, festooned with 70kg of equipment, for the same length of time in a bucking aircraft. And they must both use their controlled aggression to overcome their fear and throw themselves out the door. Relying on each other and sharing common experiences like that, even only on exercises, is bound to make the relationship between officers and men closer.

'When you ask them to do something, they are going to go and do it'

The difficulty for some officers when they first join the Regiment is that it is easy to become too friendly with the men, particularly as they are usually of a similar age, often share the same interests, and can even be from the same social background, as a senior NCO from 2 PARA relates: 'There is one officer whose head of his school house is a private soldier and in the same battalion — one is an officer, one a private soldier. The role has changed.'

But the men know just how far they can go, and the platoon sergeant guides the new subaltern in the right direction. The senior NCO from 2 PARA again: 'Of course, it is the job of the sergeant majors and the senior NCOs like myself to make sure that that bond doesn't get too close. Familiarity can breed contempt, of course, and we must ensure that that doesn't happen. But there isn't really a problem in that respect at all, since the soldier knows exactly how far to go and the officer knows how far *he* can go. We must keep that respect between officers and men.'

And that respect is mutual, because the officers realise the quality of the troops they command, and know that they are privileged to command men of The Parachute Regiment. A platoon commander who was with 2 PARA in the Falklands describes the Toms:

'They are always well-trained and naturally aggressive, probably more so than other regiments, and you don't have to worry about whether or not they are going to go and do the business. You know that when you ask them to do something, they are going to go and do it, so it actually makes your job quite a bit easier.'

'There are some people who treat the Army as a life-support system'

In fact, the aggression and motivation can cause specific problems rare in other units. A company commander from 3 PARA tells what it is like to command paratroopers:

'In some respects it is easier, and in others it is more difficult. Easier in the sense that the blokes are well-motivated, determined, strong, fit, and they will go for it. You are having to rein them in rather than push them on. The difficulty is restraining them in operations so that they are achieving the aims, or gaining and exploiting the initiative, and that is when you have to make your decision — "Do I stay where I am, or do I go on because we will achieve something better?" The other side of the coin is that it is easier in terms of motivation and all the rest of it, but harder when it comes to restraining them. In other units, the difficulty might actually be in motivating them and pushing them on in the first place. So it is a balance; it is easier in some respects and harder in others, given the nature of the man you have got.'

Commanding men of such high quality puts an added responsibility on the shoulders of a young subaltern. Élite, highly motivated and well-trained troops demand a high standard of officer to get the most from their considerable potential. No matter how good the individual Tom or NCO, the platoon as a whole must be co-ordinated in order to ensure that each man is in the right place at the right time, and covered by enough supporting fire. And an officer owes it to his men to get that right. The platoon commander from 2 PARA again:

'The big factor that the platoon commander has to be aware of is that when the bullets start flying, there are 28 or 27 little faces suddenly looking at you, as if to say: "What

Communication is vital at all levels. Here, a Tom on a live-firing exercise indicates the precise location of the 'enemy' to the other members of his section.

the hell are we going to do now?" They're waiting for your lead, for you to say, "Right, you go over there", or whatever.'

A platoon commander from 3 PARA learnt a similar lesson from eight hours under fire on Mount Longdon: 'Soldiers will do whatever is requested of them — their lives are in your hands. They will die for you if they respect you. But they will die *because* of you if you betray that trust. There are some people who treat the Army as a life-support system for their social life. In war, those people are a danger — not so much to themselves, but to their soldiers. Having seen what soldiers will do for us, I realise how privileged we, as officers, are.'

And that same officer knows what it is like to have '27 little faces suddenly looking at you': 'It was only on top of that hill that I realised the loneliness, the solitary nature of command. Many of us bluff our way — and I know I have — by leading by committee. This involves calling all your platoon staff together, getting their opinions and weighing them up before choosing a course of action. Such avoidance of responsibility was impossible that night. NCOs wanted direction, just like the Toms. And

Left: Cold, soaking, and hungry, a dog-tired Para keeps on tabbing during a very wet exercise. Life in the field is hard work, though it does have its rewarding moments.
Below: Pathfinder Platoon attacking a bridge on exercise.

they wanted it off me. I can't pretend I was an instant success, but I was all they had.'

That responsibility of command is why the officer is there. As a platoon commander from 2 PARA describes it: 'That is what you get paid for, that is the job. If you are not prepared to accept that, then you shouldn't be there. It is not really pressure at all. It is very satisfying, really it is, very satisfying.'

It is the senior officers who are ultimately responsible for standards

The Parachute Regiment relies on good officers in peace as well as war. For, along with the NCOs, the officers must organise the training, and motivate and look after the men, as well as proceed with their own professional education. And it is the senior officers who are ultimately responsible for the standards of the Regiment, since it is the officers who select the senior NCOs. A battalion can have fine senior NCOs and bad officers, and, despite the efforts of the former, the officers will often lead it to disaster. But if a regiment has good officers, then they will select and promote good NCOs. As Field Marshal Sir William Slim said: 'In the British Army, there are no good battalions and no bad battalions, no good regiments and bad regiments. There are only good and bad officers.'

MSPs AND CRAPHATS

The major responsibility of The Parachute Regiment in peacetime is for Out-of-Area operations, which can range from peacekeeping to assisting in the evacuation of British citizens abroad. To fulfil this role, they need backup — and that is where 5 Airborne Brigade comes in.

Of the three regular Para battalions, two are based at Aldershot at any one time. These units are said to be 'in role'; that is, they are doing the job of paratroopers, or training for it, rather than acting as line infantry — as part of the ACE Mobile Force, or on a two-year tour of Northern Ireland, or elsewhere in the UK in a home defence role, for example — which is how the remaining battalion is deployed.

The Para 'role' is, in fact, twofold. In the event of a general war, the two battalions would become part of the land force responsible for the defence of the United Kingdom. At all other times, they are on permanent standby for operations outside the NATO area.

The tough training programme — Recruit Company, 'P' Company and the parachute course at Brize Norton — with its emphasis on 'short, sharp, in-out' activities, makes the Paras the ideal soldiers to carry out these tasks. And, of course, their parachute capability particu-

A flight of C-130 Hercules about to take off. Just above each cockpit is the in-flight refuelling probe, giving them unlimited range if they are backed up by sufficient tanker aircraft.

larly suits them for Out-of-Area operations, where transport facilities might be limited. A senior NCO from 2 PARA gives his point of view:

'If the Government wanted something done quickly, such as the rescue of British nationals in a Third World country, or they wanted something quietened down quickly and wanted to show that they meant business, they would probably use The Parachute Regiment. Once they do so, they have let the enemy, or potential enemy, know that it isn't just someone there to hold the fort while they negotiate. When we are used, we don't go in half-heartedly. We go in for the real thing.'

However, to carry out any sort of Out-of-Area operation, the Paras need backup, since the amount of supplies and equipment that an individual soldier can take with him when he jumps from an aircraft is severely limited.

An Orders group at 5 AB Bde HQ. On the right are two officers from the US 82nd AB Div, recognisable by the 'All American ' badge on their shoulders.

Like any force going into action, to be effective they require artillery to keep the enemy's heads down, engineers to build and destroy roads and runways, mechanics for the vehicles, the vehicles themselves, medics, signals, armour, ammunition — everything, in fact, necessary to fight a successful action. For this reason, the two 'in-role' Para battalions do not operate independently, but as the spearhead of 5 Airborne Brigade, the British Army's fully mobile, rapid-deployment formation.

5 Airborne Brigade consists of two Para battalions, two airmobile infantry battalions and a full range of supporting units drawn from the other arms and services (that is, non-infantry units which do not normally wear the Red Beret). These include a regiment of artillery (18 guns), a light armoured regiment, an engineer regiment and a field ambulance unit. Like the Paras, these soldiers have to be aggressive, flexible and able to think for themselves. For, accompanying the Paras into action, they will find themselves in exactly the same situations. If they need to be dropped by parachute, they stand the same chance of

becoming separated from their commanders and they must still be able to function. Many of the soldiers who serve with the Brigade have passed 'P' Company and the 'wings' course and so feel a close bond of kinship with the Paras through membership of the so-called 'Airborne Brotherhood'. In 9 (Para) Squadron Royal Engineers, for example, each troop is assigned permanently to a particular Para battalion, so the sappers and the Toms work together all the time and get to know each other very well. Except for the two Airmobile battalions, who have their own traditions and wear their own regiment's headgear, the whole Brigade wears the Red Beret, regardless of training and courses passed, as a sign of Airborne solidarity.

The twofold role outlined above is not just that of the Para battalions; it is the role of 5 Airborne Brigade as a whole. Thus, in time of war, the Brigade would be part of the land force charged with defending the United Kingdom; in peacetime, it is responsible for planning and carrying out Out-of-Area operations — operations which can vary from helping out a friendly government, to defending a dependent territory, to serving as a peace-keeping force in a Commonwealth country.

'These are high-profile operations. You can't afford to get it wrong'

The maintenance of the Out-of-Area capability is sometimes regarded with suspicion by other branches of the Army which see BAOR as the area of prime concern. A senior officer with the Brigade, who considers a war on NATO's Central Front as unlikely, explains the importance of the Out-of-Area role in the current international climate:

'We are probably the most likely option that Her Majesty's Government is going to have in a war-type situation. It is on the peripheries, where the Superpowers have less power, where we are going to have confrontations.'

With the enormous number of British nationals living abroad, an evacuation of civilian personnel is probably the most likely type of operation that 5 Airborne Brigade, and therefore the in-role Para battalions, will be called upon to mount. A senior officer outlines a typical scenario and explains why the parachute capability might be vital:

'5 Airborne Brigade has a specific role for Out-of-Area operations, and one of the mandates is that we might have to help with the evacuation of British citizens held as hostages, or who require evacuation from a war zone, either because the local government have requested help, or because there is a breakdown in the local government and they can't protect British citizens. A lot of these countries are land-locked, and the only way of getting in there would be by air. Sometimes, we can use an airfield, but it is very easy to block an airfield, and then the only way of getting in is by parachute.'

A member of Pathfinder Platoon comes in by steerable 'chute to mark the DZ for the LPBG drop in 24 hours time. He has used the HALO technique, jumping from 18,000ft.

There are two categories of rescue operation — Services Assisted Evacuation (SAE) and Services Protected Evacuation (SPE). The former assumes that no trouble will be met in the foreign location; the Brigade would be present to supervise the embarkation of civilians and to ensure that the process of evacuation went smoothly. The latter anticipates a fight to get the British citizens — perhaps held hostage — to the planes and out of the country. It is estimated that, with the current distribution of British nationals around the globe, there are 36 countries

Members of 5 AB Brigade boarding a Hercules. The DZ flashes show 'tactical loading', where a unit is spread among several aircraft so that its men all land close to their RV.

with potential for SAE operations and a further 28 where SPE missions might be required.

Flying one, or even two, battalions of Paras halfway around the world, along with support troops, equipment and supplies, is a mammoth undertaking, whether resistance is expected or not. Thorough planning, and if possible rehearsal, is required for their to be any chance of success. As one officer says: 'These are high-profile operations, part of foreign policy to extract hostages or evacuees. You can't afford to get it wrong.' Another details some of the problems which may have to be overcome:

'We could be in two different continents, possibly three. We could be in tropical jungle, the middle of the desert, a smallish country with good facilities, or a large one — like some in West Africa — with appalling communications, a very unstable, volatile populace and a fairly inhospitable atmosphere.'

It is in situations like this that the self-reliance of 5 Airborne Brigade and the Paras is put severely to the test.

The battalions and their backup would be out on their own. The commanders must then decide what will be needed to accomplish the operation — the size of the force and the backup and equipment which must go. This is a very important consideration when everything that might possibly be required for success cannot be taken along. Anything left out must either be forgotten about, gone without, or else 'acquired' on the spot. For this reason, the Brigade is lightly equipped for a formation of its size, with as much equipment as possible designed to be air-portable.

'If all control has broken down, you might be in a situation like Entebbe'

Planning always starts with an examination of the mission — what has to be accomplished — and works backwards from there. An objective is selected for the operation and analysed; what the target is depends on the situation. A 5 Airborne officer puts forward one scenario:

'If your task is to seize and hold a method of entry and exit from the theatre of operations and the country is land-locked, your only option will be to seize an airport or, more likely, be provided with an airfield by a friendly nation. If the government [in the target country] still has control, then they can guarantee the use of an airfield and we just fly in there and land, mounting ground operations from there. If all control has broken down, you might be in a situation like Entebbe or, specifically, Kolwezi, where the Foreign Legion went in and seized the airhead.'

The size and make-up of the force to be committed and the method of delivery can then be decided. The first strike element will nearly always consist of a parachute battalion group — a full Para battalion plus support, under the command of the Para battalion CO. This force is normally referred to as the Leading Parachute Battalion Group (LPBG) because it makes the first landing ahead of the rest of the Brigade.

'Counter-attack as soon as possible, before the attackers regroup'

A decision then has to be made on how to go in — whether to carry out a Tactical AirLanding Operation (TALO) or whether to para-drop the Leading Parachute Battalion Group onto the target with what is known as 'light scales'; that is, without containers, but wearing CEFO (Combat Equipment Fighting Order — webbing), and with weapons ready for immediate use. An Airborne officer explains what influences this decision:

'In some of our operations, the airfield would be benign and in host-nation hands, and we could just land there as if we were on a passenger aircraft. On the other hand, we have various options available for taking airfields. Although we don't envisage doing that against the wishes of a host nation, if a rebel force decides to take over a capital, then the airfield is going to become the focal point. In that case, we have the option of doing a Tactical AirLanding, where we come in as covertly as possible in C-130s with people armed and ready to fire immediately they leave the aircraft and with reasonably good mobility as well. Of course, the force would be very small and vulnerable, and it would depend very much on a rapid reinforcement. That is one scenario; another is where we do the same thing but, because the runway is blocked or cratered, we would go in by parachute, which is less surgical and tends to be less refined, because you have less control over where you are and are inevitably a bit spread out. You have to concentrate yourselves, orientate yourselves, and then get on with the job in hand. Nevertheless, we are working on the skills required to drop in over the top of an airfield by basically flying straight down the runway and jumping on top of it, onto concrete.'

There is also a third option open to the 5 Airborne commanders — to parachute with containers onto an 'off-set' drop zone some kilometres away from the target. This

With the door open, the first man in the stick hangs onto his 'strop'. He has a very small container and the aircraft is comparatively empty.

does mean losing the element of surprise, since it could take two or three hours to get to the objective and put in an attack, but it also allows the troops the opportunity to rally and mount an organised assault. An Airborne officer explains the dilemma the commanders are faced with:

'The philosophy of dealing with an air parachute assault is always to counter-attack as soon as possible, before the attackers regroup. This is where it comes to this business of whether you jump onto the target or away from it. If we jump away from the target, then they might hit us before we get to the target area. If we jump on the objective, then we may have the advantage of shock action, and can seize the key objective and hold it against counter-attack. So our job is to reorganise quickly and receive and repel counter-attack.'

At this point, a tactical ground plan is drawn up, priority targets are singled out and companies, platoons and sections are earmarked to deal with them. Who is allocated what mission will eventually decide the positioning of personnel on the aircraft, with the intention that people land as close as possible to their own objective. An Airborne officer explains:

'The key areas are what the tasks are and the ground plan that comes out of that; the loading of the aircraft to

The drop goes in, as seen from the back ramp of a Hercules. Supplies (white parachutes) are dropped out of the back just before the men jump out of the sides.

meet that ground plan; crossloading — the positioning of commanders, radio operators and key equipment across the aircraft so that they are not all in one place. You then have the air plan that gets everybody over the air objective, but that is an RAF task.'

In the event of the parachuting option being chosen (considered to be the 'worst case scenario' by the commanders of 5 Airborne Brigade because it is less clinical than airlanding), members of Pathfinder Platoon are sent in 24 hours before the LPBG arrives. They parachute into the target area, free-falling from 18,000ft using the HALO (High Altitude-Low Opening) method. Their task is to recce the DZs, to see if they are still suitable for the LPBG to jump, and then to send this information back to Brigade HQ via satellite and radio links. Just before the LPBG goes in, the Pathfinders mark the DZ so that the RAF pilots know when and where to drop their 'chalks' (complements of paratroopers).

Pathfinder Platoon is made up of experienced Airborne soldiers — mostly from the Para battalions, but with some specialists from other parts of the Brigade — who have completed advanced jump courses. The Pathfinders also undergo instruction in advanced patrol techniques, because, once the Brigade is on the ground, they are employed on long-range reconnaissance missions. The platoon is what is known as a 'Brigade asset', which means that it is not attached to a battalion, but rather is tasked by Brigade HQ, going ahead of the battalions to act as the 'eyes and ears' of the Brigade.

'You have to get stuck in and use your initiative in your own way'

Twenty-one C-130 Hercules aircraft of No 1 Group RAF are required to deliver the LPBG to the DZ. Twelve of those are packed with the battalion group itself; each of the the remaining nine contain two Medium Stressed Platforms (MSPs) bearing the stores, vehicles and equipment of the support element, and the two vehicles which make up the Battalion Headquarters and Tactical Brigade Headquarters. The Brigade commander jumps in the first wave with the LPBG, thus setting up the 'one-on-one' command structure wherein the Brigadier is in overall charge and can keep the politicians and higher command off the LPBG CO's back, thus leaving him free to fight the battle. Also, by being 'on the spot', the Brigadier is better able to command the rest of the Brigade as soon as it comes in, and to make any alterations to the Brigade plan.

In operational circumstances, the aircraft approach at low level (250ft), climbing to 800ft and opening the doors two minutes out from the DZ. From the time the first Tom goes through the door, it can take as little as three and a half minutes before the whole LPBG is on the ground,

MSPs and all. Even the most disciplined of assault forces will be in some disarray directly after a parachute landing, if only for a few moments. But then, Para and Airborne training is geared towards keeping the period of uncertainty as short as possible by producing soldiers capable of acting without direct supervision. A member of 2 PARA describes what it is like dropping onto a target where the enemy is waiting — a so-called 'hot' DZ:

'When you hit the ground, everything is confusion. You have bods everywhere and you have to get yourself organised. When you hit the ground, you won't do it with the people you are working with. You have to get the people who are around you and start fighting the incident that is going on. Basically, you have to be able to work with other Airborne soldiers. You can't just say, "Well, I am nothing to do with you"; you have to be able to react and interact immediately you hit the ground. You have to get stuck in and use your initiative in your own way.'

The first objective of the LPBG is to suppress any immediate opposition and to establish an airhead, a reasonably secure point (about two square kilometres in area) through which reinforcements and resupply can be received by air. Once this has been achieved, then the LPBG must hold on to it, receiving and repelling any enemy counter-attacks. Where the target is an airfield, this amounts to capturing it, or at least clearing the runway, for the airhead has been described as the Airborne force's 'jugular vein'. When the resupply requirements are considered, it is not difficult to see why. The demand for artillery ammunition alone is colossal. Whereas the Para battalion itself, using rifles, machine guns and mortars, can last for three days on 15 one-tonne containers of ammunition, artillery rounds are so heavy and take up so much space that 22 similar-sized containers a day are required to service the three 105mm Light Guns of the LPBG's battery from 7 (Para) Regiment RHA.

'We have to be able to survive on what we can carry'

7 (Para) Regiment RHA returned to Aldershot as the resident Airborne artillery unit in 1984, after an absence of eight years on other gunnery duties. Because of the long absence engaged on non-Airborne activities, the proportion of parachutists in the regiment had declined, but now most of the unit are parachute trained and all officers and men seeking to join must pass 'P' Company. In common with the other elements which make up the LPBG, a gun

Gunners of 7 (Para) RHA placing a 105mm Light Gun onto its firing platform. In the foreground is a PRC 320, which, being HF, has a much greater range than the usual VHF radio.

Sappers from the Brigade's EOD (Explosive Ordnance Disposal) troop (shown by the red and blue DZ flash) defusing a practice bomb during an exercise. EOD proved vital 'Down South' as many Argentine bombs failed to go off.

battery is allocated to a Para battalion on a permanent basis. This, and the fact that soldiers — but not officers — can join 7 RHA at the start of their careers and sometimes remain in it throughout, helps a good working relationship to develop between the regiment and the Paras.

Of course, being a Para unit restricts the type and amount of equipment that the regiment can use. An officer with 7 RHA explains:

'Obviously, with the limitations on the amount of kit that we can bring in, we have to be able to survive on what we can carry, and technical training revolves around that. We have, for example, like all normal gun regiments, a piece of equipment that goes in the back of a Land Rover which can tell you exactly where you are. But you can't drop it out of an aeroplane, because it breaks.'

The regiment's role also determines what gun it uses

— anything larger than the 105mm Light Gun is too big to be easily para-dropped, not only in terms of the gun itself, but also because of the extra weight and size of larger-calibre ammunition.

'The only thing we don't carry is, basically, anything we can't fit in'

The role of 7 RHA is to provide artillery support for 5 Airborne Brigade. For the battery dropping with the LPBG, this means giving the Paras fire support as they knock out opposition and seek to secure the airhead. The battalion's own mortars will normally deal with the short-range targets and any counter-attack by enemy troops present on the spot. The main assistance the artillery can give is to bombard any military base within shelling range of the airhead — the 105mm Light Gun can hurl a round over 17km — with the intention of causing confusion and delaying the arrival of reinforcements. The 105mm shell, being bigger, is also better than the 81mm mortar bombs for dealing with well-protected targets, such as bunkers.

A sniper resting his L42 sniper rifle on his bergen. Laser simulator exercises and the Falklands conflict have shown the power of good snipers. Both 2 and 3 PARA were on the receiving end of very effective sniper fire 'Down South'.

Slowing down the enemy is also one of the jobs of the engineer troop attached to the battalion group. It does this through counter-mobility operations, such as blowing up roads, bridges and defiles leading to or surrounding the airfield. Like everyone else in the LPBG, the engineers are severely limited in what they can take with them to the DZ. On top of everything that they need merely to survive in the field, their bergens are packed with small tools, such as pliers, saws and wire-cutters, light drilling equipment, ropes and, of course, explosives. As a combat engineer NCO of 9 (Para) Squadron RE says, 'The only thing we don't carry is, basically, anything we can't fit in.'

Heavy plant has to be airdropped or airlanded after the first drop has gone in; the LPBG engineer troop is normally allocated, at most, two Land Rovers with trailers. This absence of heavy equipment can be a problem because the LPBG engineer troop is also responsible for clearing the runway in order to keep the airhead open. In certain circumstances, it might be possible to drop in a medium-wheeled tractor, but these vehicles take up an enormous amount of valuable aircraft space. The solution

is to 'acquire' equipment locally. This goes for vehicles as well, and a small team of Para-trained drivers from 63 Squadron RCT join the initial assault to commandeer and, if necessary, to 'hot-wire', transport in the target area.

Where no plant is to be had, Para-engineers — who, as Airborne soldiers, need to be especially well versed in military skills — slip easily into the infantry role. 9 (Para) Squadron take their Airborne role very seriously, and 70 per cent of the unit are qualified military parachutists. An NCO explains an engineer's route to 9 Squadron:

'After basic recruit training, Sappers go into combat engineer training for about 18 weeks, then they get posted to a unit. They can then volunteer to come here to us. They do pre-para with us. If they pass that, then we say to them that we think that they have more than a fair enough chance of passing "P" Company. They go and do

"P" Company, and then it is "P" Company's decision whether they pass or fail. There are about 130 people in the squadron that are para-trained. We have 175 in the squad in all, but some are non-critical storemen and aren't para-trained. The clerks are para-trained, though.'

Soldiers from corps like the Royal Engineers need to be 100 per cent certain of their desire to become para-troopers and of their ability to make it — otherwise they would be best advised not to try. As outlined above, before they even get a shot at 'P' Company they have to convince a team of instructors from their own corps that they are up to the privilege. This pre-para course is a two-week physical and mental hammering by veterans of All-Arms Pre-Parachute Selection, in recognition of the fact that men from a non-Airborne outfit, no matter how well prepared they think they are, are often not fit enough to take on 'P' Company. Joining a Para unit needs patience as well as endurance, for it usually takes around five months from arrival to becoming a fully fledged member, and this assumes that the candidate passes all the courses, from pre-para to Brize Norton, first time. This long period is because of the time spent just waiting to go on courses. The actual training involved in 'P' Company and Brize Norton takes seven weeks.

Consolidation of communications is quickly achieved

Communications are vital to any military operation. In an Out-of-Area situation, they are the vital link between the fighting sub-units of the Para battalion all the way up the command structure to Battalion Group HQ and, as such, they form a lifeline between the troops on the ground and the rear commanders. Communications within the Parachute battalions are the responsibility of signals-trained Paras. Similarly, the low-level radio nets in the support units are manned by artillery signallers, engineer signallers, and so on. But the links between the Tactical Brigade Headquarters, which is dropped with the LPBG, the rest of Brigade HQ and all the units in the Brigade are furnished courtesy of para-trained detachments from 5 Airborne Brigade's HQ and Signal Squadron, staffed by the Royal Signals.

As they hit the ground, the 'Para sigs' immediately provide Brigade Tactical HQ, to which they are attached, with HF and VHF communications. In this way, the Brigade commander is put in instant contact with the Para battalion CO, the Brigade main HQ at the secure airbase from which they have just flown, and the RAF. Also, the field commanders of the artillery battery and the engineer troop can speak to their superiors at the rear HQs of 7 (Para) RHA and 9 (Para) Squadron RE. In addition, the signals detachment opens both a UHF Tactical Air

Direction net — by means of which the Tactical Air Control Party, a small group of RAF personnel, can call down air support in the form of Harrier or Jaguar ground-attack aircraft — and a Tactical Satellite link with Brigade Rear HQ to supplement the HF and VHF connections. At this point, the LPBG is still on foot, so all the above is accomplished using manpack radio sets which the 'Para sigs' have carried down in their containers.

Consolidation of communications is quickly achieved, however, for among the vehicles dropped from the LPBG's fleet of C-130 aircraft — usually before the men themselves jump — are two 'Fitted For Radio' (FFR) Land Rovers complete with trailers. These, along with the Gunners' 105s and the Sappers' vehicles, are despatched from the aircraft by Air Despatchers of 47 (Air Despatch) Squadron RCT; this comprises the so-called 'heavy drop'. The Land Rovers contain the sets necessary to render the Brigade Command VHF net secure, and their arrival makes Brigade Tactical HQ fully mobile.

But Tac HQ will only be fully mobile if the vehicles are serviceable, and in a combat situation there are almost infinite opportunities for something to go wrong, whether it be as a result of enemy action, driver error, or simply the rough treatment involved in being dropped from an aircraft. MSPs are rigged with multiple parachutes, but parachutes sometimes fail to open, and this leads to a heavy, lop-sided landing:

'In the space of three hours they were back on the road'

'Recently, there was a drop and a couple of vehicles actually turned on their backs. Two One-Tunnies [One-Tonne Land Rovers] of the Gunners [RHA] were what *they* considered written off. They were going to take them away and we said: "No, no, this is our bread and butter." So, the fitters had bits off this one, bits off that one, and out of the two of them we made a good one. This is what we are here for; it's important to us. They had bent axles, and of course we adapted. We had chains and a jack, straightened the axles up, and off they went; in the space of three hours they were back on the road. Perhaps, from the point of view of legality on the road, it may be lacking. But look at it. It's good. This is vital, because in our particular role, we can't expect there to be a vehicle if we are in another country. The turn-around has to be pretty sharpish.'

This first aid to stricken vehicles, known as 'first-line repair' and described above by an officer of 10 Field Workshop REME (Royal Electrical and Mechanical Engineers), part of 5 Airborne Brigade's Logistic Battalion, was carried out under exercise conditions, but it is an example of the kind of task the men of the workshop's

Forward Repair Team have to perform. Apart from keeping the battalion group on the road, they have to keep it talking and firing — repairs to radio equipment and weapons are also their responsibility. Like the rest of the LPBG, they can act as infantrymen when necessary but, in the words of a REME NCO:

'The Brigade is looking to us for technical support. It might be great if we go in and all my technicians are killed being infantry but, if their radios don't work, a lot more men are going to die because they can't communicate. So, what they want from us is repair.'

Even a field operating theatre has been designed for para-dropping

In an operation as fraught with danger as a para-drop, medical help must be constantly at hand. As with communications, medical matters within the battalion are handled by soldiers of The Parachute Regiment. Regimental Medical Assistants (RMAs) carry out initial treatment at section level and casualties are then passed back up the chain of command through the Company Aid Post (CAP) to the Regimental Aid Post (RAP) where they are seen by the Regimental Medical Officer (RMO), usually a captain in the Royal Army Medical Corps (RAMC).

But casualties will probably pile up thick and fast at the RAP, as a result of fighting and of parachuting accidents, and the RMO will be in no position to do more

A Scorpion CVR(T) of the Life Guards moves forward to support a live-firing battalion night attack as the SF platoon provides covering fire from a flank.

than keep the men alive and insert a few stitches. To this end, a Medical Detachment from 23 Parachute Field Ambulance jump along with the LPBG and take on the task of putting together the wounded and injured passed to them from the RAP and holding them until they can be casevaced (casualty evacuation).

The Medical Detachment comprises a Medical Officer, eight Combat Medical Technicians (CMTs) and two Driver/Radio Operators. A surprising amount of life-saving equipment can be despatched in their containers; each man jumps carrying enough medical supplies in his bergen to treat 10 major cases. Even a field operating theatre has been designed for para-dropping. This comprises: a table, the top of which doubles as a stretcher, and all of which folds away into a large, golf-bag-type container; a ventilator, which has taken away the need to 'hand-bag' a casualty on a manual respirator; and an anaesthetic machine. Three members of the team take one article each, either in their bergens or strapped to their person. As one combat medic points out: 'You can't walk vary far with it, but it is a functional operating theatre.'

In a Service Protected Evacuation, the RAP and the Field Ambulance Medical Detachment are initially co-located at 'A' Echelon, the headquarters of the battalion group. This is because of 'lack of depth' — limited space — in the airhead. Medical care must be provided, not only for the battle casualties, but also for civilians, including perhaps women, children and old people, who are being sent back for evacuation. In addition, the Evacuee Handling Centre, which can process 150 evacuees over a 3-day period, is also at 'A' Echelon.

The follow-on infantry battalion groups are line infantry battalions

Immediately after the drop has taken place and the airhead is being established, 'A' Echelon will actually be in the same place as Brigade HQ — on the DZ. Here, the Logistics Cell of RAOC and RCT personnel who jumped in with the LPBG are busy assembling the embryonic Brigade Maintenance Area (BMA). Initially, the stores assembled here consist of the 20 tonnes of Combat Supplies (normally abbreviated to 'C' Sups) dropped on wedges and as side stores on MSPs. (A 'wedge' is a device in the back of a C-130 which allows one-tonne containers to be dropped out of the back of the aircraft while the troops are going out of the sides.) 'C' Sups are sorted and moved around with the help of an Eager Beaver, an air-portable load-shifter (MHE — Mechanical Handling Equipment) which was also parachuted in with the Logistics Cell. Over the next 24-48 hours, further drops are made of one-tonne containers, and the BMA starts to take shape. (These drops consist of 'first-line scales', the quantity of 'C' Sups officially laid-down to be held within the battalion itself. For the LPBG, these are 130 one-tonne pallet-loads.)

With the LPBG established on the ground and the airhead secure, it is now time to bring in the next element in the operation. This is the Follow Up Parachute Battalion Group (FUPBG), which has a similar make-up to the first group. Depending on the situation on the ground at the time, this group could either be para-dropped or airlanded; that is, actually set down on the runway in C-130s. While the LPBG is making the initial landing, the FUPBG is waiting at the secure airbase, known as a Forward Mounting Base (FMB).

The location of the FMB depends on where the target country for the operation is situated, and whether there are any countries friendly to Britain nearby. Where there is none, the LPBG must be flown direct from the UK into the theatre of operations. An FMB must then be established there and held until more men and supplies can be flown in. Where a friendly local country *does* exist, then an FMB can be set up at an airbase in that country. Not only can the LPBG be launched from this FMB, but also the remainder of the Brigade can assemble there, brief and rehearse, acclimatise and, finally, fly into theatre. During Operation Corporate to the South Atlantic in 1982, the FMB for the operation was Ascension Island.

Once the FUPBG is in place, and the brigade commander is satisfied that there are enough troops on the ground to hold the airhead and make a move on the objective, the actual task can begin. The company groups move forward, as does 'A' Echelon to keep in touch with its troops, taking with it the Log Cell, the RAP and Evacuee Handling Centre. Meanwhile, the major air/land operation commences, bringing in the follow-on infantry battalion groups.

The follow-on infantry battalion groups are line infantry battalions supported in much the same way as the Para battalions. They are not parachute capable, however (though they may have a nucleus of parachute qualified personnel), and therefore need to be airlanded whatever the situation. Once these have arrived, the full Brigade fighting force is on the ground. A senior 5 Airborne officer explains how these battalion groups will operate:

'You have four pretty independent battalion-group-size organisations, each between 600 and 800 strong, depending on how they are grouped. They would reasonably be expected to be given a job and to go off and act fairly independently, until they are retasked by Brigade HQ. The very nature of Out-of-Area ops is that we may be taking fairly small forces into a fairly large country, where the lines of communications are poor and the emphasis is on the battalions going away, coping on their own, and then coming back to us when they have either finished the task or have some insuperable problem.'

Everything the Brigade could want must be flown in...even water

At the same time as the later battalion groups are being airlanded, the first heavy equipment and resupply loads are being flown in as the build-up of Brigade resources at the airhead gets under way. High on the list of hardware waiting at the FMB to be airlanded would be the Scorpion light tanks and Fox four-wheeled armoured cars of the Brigade's armoured regiment, a slot shared between The Life Guards and The Blues and Royals regiments of The Household Cavalry on a two year rotation basis. The 32 Scorpions, armed with the 76mm gun, are deployed in two squadrons of 16 vehicles each, while the Fox armoured reconnaissance vehicles mount 30mm RARDEN cannons. Both types of Combat Vehicle, Reconnaissance, as the tanks and armoured cars are called, weigh in at less than 10 tonnes each and can be dropped on MSPs, which means that, if circumstances demand it, a squadron of the armoured regiment can take its place in the LPBG. For this reason, it has a core of parachute-trained officers and men.

But further ammunition for hardware already

deployed and supplies to keep the troops on their feet will also be assuming a high priority. The LPBG is sent into the field with three days' combat supplies ('Each man will get three 24-hour ration packs, his bergen, and enough ammo to keep him going and fighting in an intensive scenario.'), calculated at Limited War Rates (LWR). After this is exhausted, it is up to Brigade to find more where that came from in order to keep it fighting. If that pile of stores is multiplied by four to take account of the requirements of the other Para battalion group and the follow-on infantry battalions, it amounts to a shopping list of monumental proportions. In aircraft space alone the demands are staggering. To deliver a light force of brigade size at three days' LWR entails over 100 C-130 sorties; to deliver an all-arms brigade at seven days' LWR, over 220 sorties are needed.

Everything the Brigade could want must be flown in; and that can even mean water. In hot climates, the requirement is 20 litres per man per day. An Airborne officer explains:

'Water is something that is not always appreciated,

Officers from a Tactical Air Control Party (TACP) providing air-traffic control for aircraft bringing in the follow-up troops and supplies. A TACP also controls ground-attack aircraft.

because we spend most of our time on exercise in the UK. But we are in no doubt that, when we go to an Out-of-Area country — and most of the ones we are going to are pretty close to the equator and are either tropical jungle or desert — then water is paramount. Quite a lot of logistic effort is geared towards either producing water where we are or receiving water flown from another country and parachuted in to us.'

In some operations, four-tonne trucks are flown in

Drilling for water is another of the tasks of 9 (Para) Squadron RE, who also have a para-droppable purification kit for use on any water that is unfit to drink. But the job of receiving deliveries and controlling distribution of water and of all other supplies and equipment rests with

the follow-up contingent of the Brigade Logistic Battalion, which takes over the running of the BMA (it will cover an area of 16k/sq when fully stocked) at the airhead, and supervises the smooth flow of supplies forward.

The Logistics Battalion is equipped with a small fleet of Eager Beavers and Supacats; quite useful when it is considered that combat supplies — ammunition, POL (Petroleum, Oil and Lubricant), food and water — for the Brigade for one day amount to 1100 tonnes, all of which has to be unloaded from Hercules aircraft and stacked. An Ordnance Company soldier would be wise to keep in trim, though, for although Eager Beaver is a good machine, it still breaks down ('it is durable, but not squaddie-proof'), and then everything has to be 'humped' by hand.

In some operations, four-tonne trucks are flown in with the airland to ease the movement of supplies from the BMA to the Forward Edge of the Battle Area (FEBA), where the fighting is taking place, as the latter moves further away from the airhead. These are driven by soldiers of 63 Squadron RCT, who also provide the drivers for the vehicles of 23 Parachute Field Ambulance and the Para 'hot-wiring' teams. Damaged vehicles, and other equipment, receives 'first-line' repair on the spot where it breaks down. If this occurs at 'A' Echelon, then it is the task of the Forward Repair Teams of 10 Field Workshop REME. Anything which cannot be dealt with there must be sent back to the BMA where it is handled by the main workshop.

Everybody and everything necessary can be brought in by aircraft

Battlefield support to the Brigade is provided by the six Scout and six Gazelle helicopters of 658 Squadron AAC. But, as distances between the airhead and 'A' Echelon and the front increase, it may be necessary to use helicopters to deliver supplies and to bring out casualties and evacuees. Since the AAC helicopters are too small for this task, it is performed by RAF Chinook and Puma helicopters which are taken to pieces and flown into the theatre of operations in C-130s. Loads are taken to 'A' Echelon slung underneath the choppers and put down at a Landing Site nearby. Sometimes, the C-130s themselves will make supply drops, flying over a Stores DZ — a dropping zone marked out at 'A' Echelon for supply runs only — and dropping as much as 16 tonnes of stores in one pass.

Everybody and everything necessary for a successful operation can be brought in by aircraft. But the airland phase — which, once started, is in progress continuously

A Chinook support helicopter of 7 Sqn RAF moving a Land Rover and trailer forward from the BMA. The Chinook can carry 11,300 kg in underslung loads, or 44 troops.

throughout the operation — need not be the end of the story as far as reinforcement and resupply of the Brigade goes. In the event of a protracted campaign in a country which is accessible from the sea, there is a contingency known as 'Seatail', whereby very large items, such as heavy recovery vehicles, and 'cosmetic' items, such as bumpers and wing-mirrors, can be brought by ship.

Swift, 'smash-and-grab' missions, employing the element of surprise

Where sea-borne landings are possible — for example, in an evacuation operation — there might be a link-up with 3 Commando Brigade. In such a scenario, 5 Airborne Brigade would go in first to find and secure the UK nationals. The Commando Brigade would then come in to reinforce, establishing a beachhead through which both 5 Airborne and the evacuees would be shipped out.

Fundamentally though, the Airborne and Commando forces are quite different instruments. The former is intended essentially for swift, 'smash-and-grab' missions, employing the element of surprise to offset their light equipment scales. The latter is used for heavier, sea-borne assaults, where surprise is less important because of the numbers of helicopters and the weight of logistics at their disposal, which an Airborne force could not possibly carry.

Theoretically, 5 Airborne Brigade is on 5 days standby to embark on an Out-of-Area operation. In fact, the period of notice to move could be much shorter. In order to meet this requirement, they have a tough training schedule. An Airborne officer itemises the annual programme:

'In any given year, we can bank on having major exercises which involve the bulk of the Brigade and are geared towards covering two or three of the following aspects.

Brigade HQ is on exercise seven or eight times a year

'First, Brigade competitions, where we are using the competition as a catalyst for soldiers increasing their proficiency at low-level, individual skills. This is along the lines of general military skills which anyone in the military should be expected to know. Second, live firing exercises at battalion level, where we get as close as we can to replicating an actual battle by using all of the integral infantry weapons and support weapons within the Brigade, including artillery, armoured reconnaissance, and involving engineers and building in fighter ground-attack. This requires an awful lot of co-ordination and has heavy overheads, but the benefits are well worth while. Thirdly, exercises which practise the Brigade mounting concept by air, and inevitably involving parachuting.'

On top of this come Field Training Exercises (FTXs)

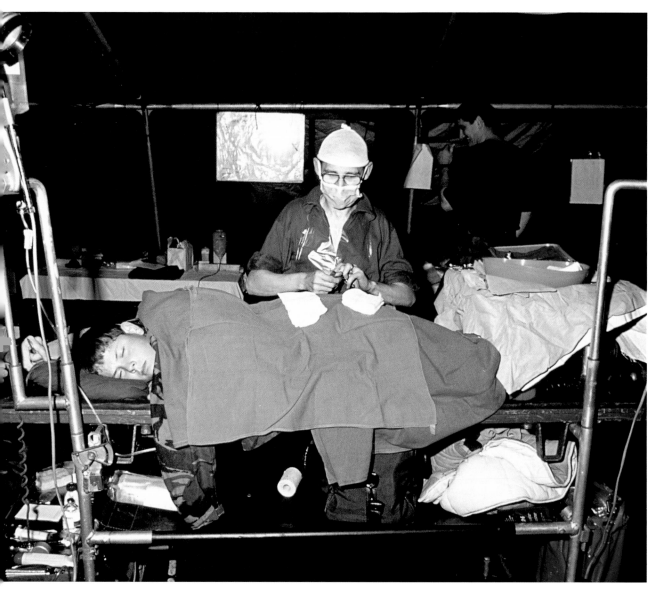

**A Field Surgical Team from 23 Parachute Field Ambulance.
The complete operating theatre can be air-dropped, each
medic involved jumping with a table, anaesthetic machine
or ventilator in his bergen.**

where elements of the Brigade are sent out into the field
to 'play soldiers'. That is the agenda for the year as far as
Brigade training is concerned, but there is more. The
Airborne officer continues:

'The Brigade HQ also sponsors four or five exercises a
year where battalions are being exercised but, because of
the problems of actually mounting a parachute battalion
with its supporting elements by air, it needs Brigade HQ

to be involved. So, Brigade HQ is on exercise seven or
eight times a year, and units within the Brigade about the
same amount. Two of them on major brigade deploy-
ments, and the rest on exercises of their own.'

This heavy schedule can play havoc with a soldier's
outside life, but those who are subject to it see it as
preferable to other postings in the Army, as is confirmed
by an NCO of 9 (Para) Squadron RE:

'Well, you could probably sum it up by the fact that if
you are married, you see your wife on Sunday, you take
your dirty washing home, and you tell her to get it washed.
The next day you are off again. About 200 days a year; you
are not home very often. All right, you are only an hour

and a half away from Aldershot, but it is still away from home. You aren't there very often in the year. Because we are away from home most of the year, the married and single soldiers don't treat each other as married and single soldiers, they just work as a team. If you stay in camp too much, then the split comes; it becomes a civilian job. You knock off at half past four and...you know...'

However, although the Brigade exercises together and works well as a team, it would be wrong to suggest that there is no friction or rivalry between units. A major bone of contention is the right to wear the coveted Red Beret.

'It's a real sickener to see a woman with a Red Beret on'

5 Airborne Brigade is, as its title proclaims, an Airborne brigade; it is not a Parachute formation. The majority of the Brigade is para-trained; the Para battalions are, of course, fully so, and units such as 9 (Para) Squadron RE and 7 (Para) Regiment RHA, which have 70 per cent of their personnel wearing Para 'wings', also belong to the so-called 'Airborne Brotherhood'. The other elements of the Brigade have a proportion of their strength qualified in order to support the LPBG, or mount recce operations, but the remainder of their personnel have undergone training in airlanding techniques only; they have not done 'P' Company or Brize Norton.

In order to instil a feeling of unity within the British Airborne Forces it was decided that all members of 5 Airborne Brigade would be allowed to wear the Red Beret of The Parachute Regiment while they were serving with the Brigade, regardless of whether they had undergone any special training or not. But, just presenting a man with a Red Beret does not suddenly turn him into the type of soldier needed for Airborne operations; he has first to show that he has those Airborne attributes. Once upon a time, the Red Beret was presented to recruits in the Paras when they passed off the square after six weeks of training, but in recent years it has been the reward for passing the legendary 'P' Company. Thus, the practice of presenting 'craphats' (or 'hats' for short) with Red Berets simply for being posted from a desk job in BAOR, when it takes a Para several months of unmitigated torture, has not been universally welcomed. Of course, the Paras have an excellent relationship with 9 Squadron and 7RHA, where those who join are soon sent through 'P' Company and are among the recipients of the coveted Red Beret, and it is the 'desk johnnies' who are most despised. While the Paras would not dispute that these soldiers are good at their jobs and indispensable to the operational efficiency of the Brigade, there is resentment at what they see as a devaluation of a symbol. An NCO from a Para battalion gives vent to his feelings:

'What we hate, and everybody in the Brigade will agree, is the amount of "hats" that have got the Red Beret. Parachuters have the Red Beret, but down there in Brigade Ordnance you have a bunch of wasters who are going around in the Red Beret and giving us a bad name. In a brigade you do need supporting arms, but when you see guys — big, fat, useless things — walking around town posing with the Red Beret on, it makes you sick, because *you* earn it. When you are in the Depot, you are proud when you get that beret. But the worst thing was when women started wearing them; getting attached to the unit and actually wearing one of the Red Berets. It was sickening to see, especially when civvies, who only know certain things, say, "Well, a woman wears it so it can't be that good." It's a real sickener to see a woman with a Red Beret on. I mean, if someone is attached they should keep their own berets and make some distinction about it.'

However, the issue of berets apart, the Paras and their colleagues in 5 Airborne Brigade do function as an effective force. Whether Para or airland, when they are thousands of miles from home in an unknown country, all the links in the chain must show the same amount of competence and initiative, regardless of headgear, or the chain will snap. An Airborne officer sums up why:

'It is a case of initiative at all levels, which is ideal for parachutists'

'We are quite likely to be a very small force in quite a large country, dealing with issues that are well spread out. If you take a Services Protected Evacuation, for example, which is just one of our roles, you are talking about sending fairly small groupings of troops — battalion groups or just a company group, perhaps only 150 people — off with some helicopters into the area without really knowing what is going on, with only a very hazy picture. Hence, initiative and independence of action — coordinated by us but not gripped tightly by us — is very much the order of the day. That is the way we have to play it. It is all geared towards "Right, there is the kit. There is the task. Those are the constraints. Give us a shout telling us about your progress and any problems you may have, and come back when it's over." Rather than being given a job and then, before you have really found out what it is, you are being told how to do it, and then, when you start to do it, it is being done for you by some bugger who won't get off your back. We can't do that in this brigade even if we want to, because we just have too many balls in the air, and are too far spread out. The communications are too stretched. So it is a case of initiative at all levels, which is ideal for parachutists, because they tend to be quite self-centred individuals, in a funny sort of way, although they can operate in a team as well.'

READY FOR ANYTHING

Utrinque paratus **is the motto of The Parachute Regiment, and they do their best to live up to it. This means hard training, with as much of it as possible under realistic conditions, and doing their share of tours of duty in foreign parts. It all adds up to plenty of travel, and the chance to let their hair down in some unusual places.**

The Para motto, which translates as 'Ready for Anything', is apt, considering the Regiment's role in the modern British Army. Two of its three battalions are on constant stand-by for Out-of-Area operations. In addition, like all British infantry units the Para battalions do tours in Northern Ireland and Belize, and serve with the United Nations peacekeeping force in Cyprus; they also have a Home Defence role should the need arise. So it is not surprising that the Paras' training and exercise programme is hectic, nor that the old saying 'Join the Army and see the world' is, in their case, still current.

The problem with preparing for Out-of-Area operations is that no-one can know with any certainty where the next incident will occur, or what shape it will take. It could be peacekeeping in a city or the desert, or fighting in near-polar or tropical conditions. Wherever and whatever the situation, however, the in-role Paras must be ready to deploy at short notice and fit to fight upon arrival; it is unlikely that there would be much time for

A Para section advances through a stream during a live-firing exercise in the Sennybridge training area in Wales.

acclimatisation. Each environment throws up its own operational snags, and it is only by working in these conditions and experiencing the difficulties first-hand that the confidence to cope with them can be gained. So, out of the five months that the Paras spend away from barracks every year, around half are devoted to giving them experience in as many climates and environments as possible.

Conditions could not be much further removed from those of Northwest Europe than in Kenya, where the British Army uses a number of areas grouped around Mount Kenya for arduous training, in environments ranging from arid desert to humid rainforest, with mountainous country in between. In Kenya, the Toms work at altitudes where the lack of oxygen can knock the wind out of the fittest man after a few hundred yards — and that is only at walking pace.

The varied Kenyan terrain allows a battalion to set up a camp and then disperse to the various areas to cover specific aspects of training. A Para officer sets the scene:

'The nucleus was the battalion base. We then had Mpala Farm to the north, and Doldol — which is very barren and dry and inhabited by local tribes — for dry training [that is, using blank rounds]. Then there was an enormous great desert area, Archer's Post, which was used by the support weapons; we dropped into there and did the main battalion live-firing exercise. Then, around the southern side of Mount Kenya are two jungly areas — it's always termed jungle, but it's certainly not your far-eastern jungle. I mean, some people reckon it's just a good English forest with the temperature turned up very, very high, but it's ideal for practising navigation and that sort of thing. It's all a relatively small area, but it's got all the different environments you could wish for, so it's absolutely ideal in that respect.'

The Kenyan jungle brings its own dangers and discomforts

Over a six-week exercise in such unfamiliar surroundings, plenty of novel difficulties present themselves. In temperatures well over 100 degrees fahrenheit, dust and thirst are twin demons, with water always warm and in constant demand. Also, keeping up lines of communication in mountainous country tests the signals platoon and the supply experts, especially since the latter may have to rely on locally acquired transport, in the form of camels and donkeys. Other large, and often unfriendly, animals can also be encountered during river crossing exercises, and the Kenyan jungle brings its own dangers and discomforts, as a member of 1 PARA points out:

A MILAN missile operator from 1 PARA takes to his skis during winter warfare exercises in Norway. Such training was a regular feature of the battalion's stint with the AMF.

'Once you go in, you're obviously stuck under the canopy. Sometimes you catch a bit of light, but with all the moisture in there, the deeper you go, well...You may catch some light now and then, but after a month or so you could come out looking quite yellow. Some of the rats were maybe a foot long, and they used to try and pull your bergen away, or tried to eat your food through your bergen, so we put the bergens up in the trees. Well, if the rats were in arm's reach, we used to hit them with a spade, and some used to try and shoot them. And if you fell asleep — one of the lads had a rat cuddled up where his legs were bent while he was sleeping. He was woken up by the sentry, and there was a rat sleeping, trying to catch some warmth off the back of his legs. Generally, people found that if they were cut, then it was hard, being in moisture all the time, to get fungicides or bandages or plasters onto the wet wounds. You used to have to take them out and get them dried off, and maybe get them casevaced.'

Desert fieldcraft is another skill that must be mastered

However, the Toms still seem to enjoy the jungle, but they 'didn't like to stay there a lot, because after a week or so you start to get the fleas etc, and the Toms would rather get out in the heat where they could run around.'

And at some point in the visit, they will be able to run around in the heat on one of the Army R&R (Rest and Recreation) arrangements. These figure highly in some trips abroad, where a year's hard graft is rewarded with a chance to let off steam. Indeed, though work is taken as seriously as ever, the holiday atmosphere even extends to some soldiers being accompanied by their wives, who can fly out and stay at one of the base camps.

Some Toms may also elect to go on safari, courtesy of the Army; others may choose to climb Mount Kenya. A soldier from 1 PARA outlines another of the options:

'They had a week's package down at Lake Naivasha. It had fishing, windsurfing, water-skiing, and other trips you could do if you wanted to: you could go climbing on day trips from the R&R centre. It was a good week in all; most people enjoyed that.'

Kenya is only one of a number of places the British Army goes to teach its soldiers how to deal with extreme climates. Desert training, for instance, is also carried out in the Sultanate of Oman on the Arabian Gulf, as well as in Kenya. A corporal in 1 PARA describes the conditions:

'In the Oman, I found, where you have the jebel, the mountainous terrain, you can be on plain desert land or semi-desert, and you can travel for 10 miles on flat ground, and within the next mile you can come to a plateau that reaches 10,000 feet, and on the other side it will be flat again for another 10 miles and the same left and right — and we always used to find the big plateaux.'

One of the major points that needs to be learnt whenever a force is operating outside its normal environment is what kit should be carried in the bergen, and what a soldier can get away *without* carrying. A veteran of an exercise in Oman gives an inventory of his bergen in a country where thirst is as effective a weapon as a rifle:

'We took doss bags, but it's a piece of kit you don't really need in the desert. There is a lot you don't need in the desert. You don't need boot cleaning kit because the sand keeps them clean, and you don't have all the warm clothing and gumpf. You need nothing in your bergen but a lightweight blanket and water. You carry as much water as you can, depending on how long you're out for. If it's for over a day, then at least four water bottles. Two or three days, and it depends on how many water bottles you have. You soon get used to travelling that way.'

Desert fieldcraft is another skill that must be mastered. While the same basic principles apply in any terrain, it is important to practise camouflage, concealment and

movement in arid country. In such terrain, for example, much can be achieved with just a few pieces of hessian. These can be placed over a position to provide not only concealment from the air, but also to act as a sunshield. And the ground is often too hard to dig in very far, so you dig in a bit and then build up a wall of rocks known as a sangar. Also, there's no need to toil over digging out squares of turf to camouflage the chalky spoil from the bottom of your trench as there would be on Salisbury Plain. An SNCO from 2 PARA explains:

It is usual for the Paras to undergo some form of special-theatre training

'The desert is that rocky in some places that you can just set yourself up a little sangar and stand back and you can't see it. All the sand and everything around is all the same colour; the topsoil is the same there as deeper down, and you can actually dig a long way without having to worry about the spoil.'

But there are also dangers to living in the desert. A corporal from 1 PARA describes desert anti-wildlife drills:

'The guys gave their boots the odd shake and, obviously, undid the sleeping bag and gave that a rattle. One of the lads was caught by a scorpion. A lad in the mortar platoon;

Skis are the most efficient way of getting about on land in the Arctic conditions of Norway. Here a Para ski patrol sets out.

he was stung. Simple things like going to the toilet: you had to check it first, make sure there were no rats in it.'

Wherever the British Army goes, there is the danger of antagonising the local populace and its feelings. This is particularly true in places like Kenya and Oman, where the local customs and habits are quite alien to the visiting soldiers, whose thoughtlessness can cause friction. This can be avoided, however, as a corporal with 1 PARA explains:

'In the [Kenyan] mountains, you had to let the people accept you before you went near them. Like we used to go to the villages and do a spot of medical work when we weren't working with the companies, and try and get the people's confidence. And if they'd let us, we used to clean the kids' wounds up if they had any. On the whole, the people used to come up to us and find out what we were doing. There was no friction between us and the locals, and the same again in Oman when we were there. You'd have to call for a guide to see you into the village, because of the women and the religion.'

Although the 'worst case Out-of-Area scenario' pictures the Paras parachuting into a hostile reception on the

other side of the world, with the minimum — if any — preparation, in circumstances that are less than absolutely desperate some measure of rehearsal or even just acclimatisation could be expected. Thus, when a major overseas exercise, or an operational tour, is in the offing, it is usual for the Paras to undergo some form of special-theatre training. The corporal from 1 PARA explains:

Airdrops with the host forces is a customary part of overseas visits

'It would be different working in a hot environment if you didn't work up to it. Obviously, before we go to California, and before we go anywhere special, we get a package together to get the lads into the frame of mind, including the kind of temperature they will be dealing with. So when they get there, they acclimatise over a three- or four-day period — do some running in the morning, running in the evening, so when it comes to the exercise, they're fit and ready for it.'

1 PARA went to California early in 1989 to take part in Exercise Caltrop Force, along with host US troops and other visitors from Canada and Australia. In addition to gaining extra desert experience, they also had the opportunity to jump with the US Airborne Forces, using the US

A member of 1 PARA lies wounded in the snow with his leg blown away above the knee. His horrific 'wounds' are, in fact, realistic make-up as he is a simulated casualty on AWT.

A Para NCO on training in Cyprus signals to his patrol to come up. He is wearing the lightweight combat uniform used by the British Army in warm climates, and carries an SA 80.

T-10-B service parachute. Taking part in airdrops with the host forces is a customary part of overseas visits, but it is not only a 'jolly', it has its serious and practical side as well. The Para officer explains why:

'It's a good experience for the lads to jump with a 'chute that they haven't used before, and to have faith in it. The T-10 'chute is very workable, and we were jumping it with our own equipment. That was simple, a piece of pie, in comparison with, say, the French at Kolwezi, who ended up jumping with equipment that belonged to the Zairean Army and with Zairean aircraft. The French hadn't left their 'chutes behind, but they'd put them far lower down the priority to come out, because they were still getting troops out when the whole thing changed, and they had to go in in such a hurry they never got a chance to get hold of their own. So they hadn't forgotten them or anything, they just needed to move quicker, and they went for what was a classic improvisation of what was there, and it worked. So it's useful to jump with other

people's equipment and have a bit of faith in it, because nobody makes a parachute that doesn't work. They all work and in their own sweet way, and they test them as thoroughly as the next man.'

Dropping with the US forces meant not only that the Paras used US 'chutes, but also that they came into contact with US parachuting drills. The Para officer again:

'It's quite awe-inspiring to come out of what is really a jet'

'The parachuting was a good experience for the guys, because the drills and everything are very different from the drills that we do here. There is far more macho shouting and things in the back of the aircraft, so there was quite a lot of ribbing and humour, because it is not something we do. I think the Americans are quite honest as to why they do it: it overcomes the fear and gets the group feeling and identity going, whereas we probably go quieter, and that's *our* way of getting together. We learned one specific thing: the Americans do actually tend to wear their equipment for the duration of the flight. Of course, they don't carry nearly as heavy or bulky loads as we do.'

Flying all the way to the DZ wearing their enormous containers was the first new experience for 1 PARA; the second was jumping from the standard US parachuting aircraft, the C-141 Starlifter, a different proposition to the familiar C-130 Hercules of No 1 Group RAF. The Para officer again:

'It's a different experience to exit from the 141, going out at a considerably faster speed. It's quite awe-inspiring to come out of what is really a jet. It's very different from a C-130, so it was good experience to do a daytime practice and a nighttime exercise jump. The jumping speed of a Hercules is 120-125 [knots], and in the 141s we were up to about 140, which is actually a significant increase, and therefore you are not meant to force your way out, you should just get out and get caught by the wind and go down. We forgot that once and it led to a lot of us getting in twists on the first jump. In a Hercules, you want to make a positive step out, so it was a reversal.'

'Working in the Arctic was very challenging because of the temperature'

The basic tactics that the Paras use in warm countries are the same as those that they would employ in Europe. Indeed, the Paras try to stick to the same principles wherever they are. An exception is when they are operating in the Arctic, though even here it is not so much a change in tactics but in their application. The 1 PARA corporal, who was with the battalion when they served with the Allied Command Europe's (ACE) Mobile Force, spending much of their time in Norway and Denmark, outlines the changes and what they were up against:

'The same tactics were applied where possible. However, everything was slowed down because of the conditions and temperatures and snow coming up to your waist — simple things, like preparing to move to another location. Over here, it generally takes about two minutes, from when you get the word to tabbing off down the road. In Norway, it was obviously a different case; some temperatures are minus 20. If you're moving at night you take up to a good hour, hour and 15 minutes, to take the tent down, make sure everything is prepared to move, get everybody together, then get off. We slowed everything down because of the temperature.

'Working in the Arctic was very challenging because of the temperature. In some cases it went down to minus 45 with the chill factor, even minus 70. But at minus 30 you should pull the zip down on your tent, for safety reasons. But some people did work out in colder temperatures, like if they were on patrol. We used to generally do OP [Observation Post] work and forward reconnaissance, and then give the information back to the battalion as normal.'

But sojourns abroad are not all brief trips for training

Paras serving with the United Nations peacekeeping force in Cyprus (UNFICYP) on OP duty. During their service with the UN, the Paras temporarily trade in the familiar Red Beret.

Paras disembark from an RAF C-130 Hercules on a desert airstrip during Exercise Swift Sword. This was an Out-of-Area exercise, in which 3 Commando Brigade also took part.

exercises. Visits to Belize take the form of a six-month short tour as resident British infantry battalion — unaccompanied by families — during which the battalion is spread around the various British Army locations, from Airport Camp in the north to Salamanca in the south.

The Army role in Belize is to defend it from neighbouring Guatemala, which lays claim to the country. It is therefore an operational tour, and is normally carried out by the out-of-role Para battalion, as part of their cycle as a conventional infantry battalion. The job includes manning frontier OPs, patrolling, training the Belizean Defence Force (BDF), and making friends and fostering good relations with the local population. A Para describes what the job entails:

'The Guatemalans were next door and they were always threatening to come over into Belize and overrun it and what have you, so we were there as a deterrent basically. In fact, all we were doing was doing patrols, keeping the Guatemalans at bay on one side and keeping the Belizeans on *their* side. That's all we were doing, just patrolling, nothing else, because they have their own force, the BDF. And we did defence exercises, things like that.'

During this tour, which took place in 1984, there was

no fighting along the border with Guatemala — 'They observed us and we observed them; that's all it was' — but there was still the heat and the threat of disease, and worse, to contend with. Life in the jungle is very uncomfortable, as the same Tom explains:

'You couldn't sleep on the ground because of snakes, so you got yourself off the ground in a hammock. But you couldn't really settle in because it was so hot. B Company location was about another 10 miles up the road from our location, and they had no water up there. I mean, it was like a drought. They were having to come down. We had enough water to spare, but we were limited on the water we could have for showering. We were limited to one period a day, or perhaps two periods a day, of 10 minutes. We were on water rations, really.'

'There was another young bloke who got bitten by a snake'

But intense heat and lack of water were nothing compared with what *could* happen. The Para again:

'There was an incident with a 2 PARA lad who was out there in the jungle before us. It was what they call a rhino beetle. They are big beetles and they've got horns on them like rhinos, and they fly. Bloody big horrible things they are. This bloke came in with a fractured skull. He got

A Para GPMG team in position during Exercise Swift Sword. The Paras nicknamed this gun the 'Widowmaker' when it made its debut in the Radfan campaign of the 1960s.

hit by one. He got casevaced out. There was another young bloke who got bitten by a snake. He was bitten outside the camp cookhouse, and by the time he had run down to the guardroom, which was only 100 metres away, he was dead.'

'It had three little pubs and the local brothel, and that was it'

As far as possible, battalion routine carries on as it does at home, with those not on operational duties participating in training exercises. Even preparation for NCO cadres goes ahead, although windswept Brecon no doubt comes as something of a shock after training runs through the steaming rainforest. The daily programme in Belize, on the other hand, is quite different to what the Paras are used to at home. For a start, work finishes at lunchtime, and apart from guard duties and the like, a soldier's time is his own. This does not make Belize a dream posting, however, as the Para explains:

'Because it's so hot out there, we were stood down at lunchtime. At midday down there you're talking about temperatures of 110. You can imagine working in that — it's horrendous. Also, there's nothing to do in the evening. Not a damn thing. We were down in the south sector and there was nothing for us to do at all at night. Up at Airport Camp, which is in the north sector, they were OK, because there's a bit more to do at night. But we were in a small little camp in the middle of the jungle. The nearest town was a little shanty place built on stilts, three miles down the road on the edge of the sea. And that was it. It had three little pubs and the local brothel, and that was it. I mean, there was *nothing*.

'The main dish down there was fish, obviously. They all used to go out on the quays fishing and come back with the fish. You could get some nice cooked meals and that in the pubs at night. The order of the day was the local drink — charcoal rum, my favourite. And that was the highlight of the night. What the lads used to do was go out running in the evening, let it cool down a bit, watch the television, then go and get bloody sloshed in the NAAFI; put back the body fluids that were lost during the day. It was a never-ending circle. I lost two stone in weight.'

Sweating it out in the remote Belizean jungle does have its advantages, however. Apart from the customary inter-unit sports competitions, the location offers sailing in the Caribbean during off-duty times, and R&R trips to Miami and other parts of the nearby United States.

The British Army's contribution to international peace-keeping is not confined to Central America. Since the Turkish invasion of Cyprus in July 1974, the United Nations has maintained a peacekeeping force (UNFICYP) on the island. Its main role is to monitor the Green Line, the winding frontier between the Greek and Turkish sectors, which is manned by troops of many nationalities, including British. The infantry element of the British contingent (Britcon) is normally drawn from one of the resident battalions responsible for the security of the two British Sovereign Base Areas (SBAs), and the Paras, once again in their capacity as an infantry regiment, are called upon to carry out this duty when they find themselves stationed on the island. The Tom sets the scene:

'You were constantly alert, because the Turks used to do funny things at night'

'I was in Redoubt Camp, and just down on the south side of Nicosia was Blue Beret Camp — engineers, Canadians; the Swedes were further up the line. It was split into sectors all the way down the line — British, Canadian and Swedish. It was funny, because in Nicosia, with us being UN troops, we could go over the border into the Turkish sector. Things were so bloody cheap over there. I used to go over at a place called the Ledra Palace. The Ledra Palace is one of the highest buildings on that side of Nicosia, and on the roof they had a cafe and bar, and you could look right across the valley where the Turks jumped in when they invaded. The DZ's still there, with remnants of the actual battle. Obviously, Nicosia's like that all round: aircraft that have not been moved and things like that. Apparently, there is still a hangar on the old Nicosia airfield, and in there they've still got planes and various bits of equipment from the war. It's there, just on the UN side.'

Cutting straight across the Green Line, bisecting it at several points guarded by Greek, Turkish and UN checkpoints, is a piece of no-man's-land known as the 'Corridor'. It is closed to other British troops on the island but, as part of the UN soldiers' task is to man the checkpoints, they have the run of this particular stretch of road. The Tom again:

'All the checkpoints are interwoven. We'd leave Nicosia, and instead of going the long way round to get back up to Dhekelia, we'd go up the Corridor, which was the short route. We went through a British checkpoint first, then a Canadian, then a Greek, another Greek, then a Turkish, and finally another Turkish.'

Although Cyprus is a holiday island, life for the troops

Paras on UN duty patrol the demilitarised zone between the Turkish forces and the forces of the Republic of Cyprus. Note the UN flag attached to the signaller's radio antenna.

is far from relaxing. In addition to manning vehicle check-points (VCPs) on the Corridor, Britcon is responsible for the OPs in the British sector. Here, face to face with the Turkish Army, the hours are long and the work often very tedious. In the Mediterranean sunshine it can be difficult to remain vigilant, but it is important. The Para again:

'You were constantly alert, because the Turks used to do funny things at night. Down the Corridor you've got the barrels [for marking boundaries]; they'd move them forward about 20 or 30 feet. But we'd know and we'd go and put the bloody things back. Each time they used to try and gain that little bit of land. Some of the lads on the line were working stag on, stag off. They went out for a full week, a section of them inside this little roofed sangar thing. They used to go out and stag on for two hours at a time between them, two blokes at any one time for a full

A Blowpipe team attached to 5 Airborne Brigade advances across the desert during Exercise Swift Sword in Oman. The oncoming soldier carries an SLR with BFA.

to make the most of what spare time came their way. Fortunately, Cyprus has a lot to offer in terms of relaxation. The weather is good, food and drink is reasonably cheap, and there are beaches with girls. One in particular, near the village of Ayia Napa, is somewhat irreverently nicknamed 'Nipple Beach'. The Tom reminisces:

'When you got your day off — if you got one at the weekend you were lucky — you could nip up to Larnaca, near Dhekelia Sovereign Base. Just further up the coast was a place called Ayia Napa. We used to go up at weekends just to relax, to get away for a day. We used to get there in the morning about half nine, and stay till about four o'clock, then come back down to Redoubt. It was a good two hour journey back for us. If we got back in time, we'd have a barbecue at night. We never used to bother with the evening meal because it was so hot, and we'd have a barbecue outside our own little bar. It was called the Pauper Inn, because everybody in there was always poor.'

The streets of Northern Ireland offer a different challenge

Naturally, the Toms are fond of their active and globetrotting life-style. As the 1 PARA corporal says: 'Given a week or two after being back in the lines [Montgomery Lines, Aldershot] and doing guards and duties, they always like to get back out on exercise; and whenever the odd foreign trip comes up, well...'

But, these being basically working visits, 'seeing the world' is not all glamour. As a 1 PARA Tom puts it: 'It's basically just the same as being over here, except you're in a different country. It's the same work.' For instance, when companies from the Regiment go to Cyprus on exercise, they train in the hot and dusty areas of the east of the island. Tabbing up steep mountains or through river valleys under the fierce midday sun, with the straps of their laden bergens digging painfully into their shoulders, the Toms soon yearn for the familiar, rolling hills of cool Salisbury Plain. But when ENDEX (END of EXercise) comes, and the Toms get a few days of water-skiing, windsurfing and LOB (Lying On the Beach), then they wish they could stay.

The main reason for exercises to Cyprus is to train in difficult climate and terrain. But it does have the advantage that for much of the time at least one Parachute Regiment company is acclimatised to heat, is training together as a team with no distractions, and is much closer to where it might be needed than it would be in Montgomery Lines. This is a company which is very much 'Ready for Anything'.

A 1 PARA Tom waiting to emplane during Exercise Caltrop Force in California. On his back he is wearing the US T-10 main parachute.

week, then they'd go back to the Box Factory and have a break. It wasn't much of a break; they were still carrying out duties, normal parading. Then back out again, and they did that for three months. In fact, some of them went out and actually stayed in a location for three months — stag on-stag off for three months. They used to work it between themselves when they could wangle a day off each. They had to have a break. Well, logging everything all the time, they could tell you that drum wasn't there last night, it was over there. They knew everything. It was like sitting in your back yard and watching your neighbour; that's just what it was like out there. You were OP'ing all the time. All the bloody time.'

Working such a demanding shift system, the Paras had

A 1 PARA MILAN team at their post during exercises with US forces in California. On their bodies and helmets are sensors for the MILES weapons' effects simulator.

A patrol from 1 PARA moves through a shallow stream during Exercise Caltrop Force in California. The red DZ flash denoting 1 PARA is clearly visible below the Para wings.

The streets of Northern Ireland, scene of Britain's longest-running military campaign this century, offer a different challenge to the Paras than do Belize or Cyprus. Service in the Province is now part and parcel of joining the Army, especially an infantry regiment, and despite the intensive training beforehand and living under a constant threat once there, it is welcomed by many soldiers as a chance to do their job for real. This is not blood lust — there is far more to soldiering than killing — it is simply a wish to put professional skills and training to the test. Others find Northern Ireland frustrating. Although the possibility of danger is ever present, the monotony is a reality and some Paras would much rather be doing 'real' soldiering somewhere else. But it is a financially lucrative tour. With Northern Ireland pay on top of usual

rates, as well as few places and little time to spend the money, a Tom can save about £2000 from his pay on a four-and-a-half-month tour. A group from 1 PARA rode motorcycles down through California after Exercise Caltrop Force, and blew all their Northern Ireland savings in Disneyland.

The Regiment has had its share of suffering and controversy

Since 1969, when the present round of 'troubles' began, the three regular battalions of The Parachute Regiment have served well over 20 tours of Northern Ireland between them. This includes tours of both the four-and-a-half-month 'roulement' variety, under Operation Banner, the official codename for the internal security operation in Northern Ireland, and the two-year residential type. During the course of these tours, the Regiment has had its share of suffering — in particular the incident at Warrenpoint in

1979, when 16 men from 2 PARA were killed by two terrorist bombs. It has also had its share of controversy, notably on 'Bloody Sunday' in 1972. At the end of an emotionally charged day of Republican marches and riots, 13 civilians died when members of 1 PARA opened fire in Londonderry. The Paras are adamant they were fired on first, and the official inquiry exonerated them.

Today, the Paras are sent to Northern Ireland on rotation as just any other infantry regiment. In common with other units, they undergo pre-tour training at one of the NITAT (Northern Ireland Training Advisory Team) centres to prepare them. For though Northern Ireland is an operational theatre, a Tom is not taught how to act in the special conditions of the Province during his time at Depot.

During NITAT training, units benefit from over 20 years of accumulated Army experience in Northern Ireland. The training is based on the principle of 'Why learn from your own mistakes when you can learn from the mistakes of others?' — particularly when a mistake may cost you your life. The Paras are also brought up to date on what to expect in the Province, and the latest techniques for dealing with it. They are taught what to look for, what to do and what not to do, and how to stay alive. Practice patrols are punctuated by staged demonstrations and bar-room fights, with other soldiers taking the part of protesters and brawlers. In the quest for realism, 'rent-a-crowd', as these mock demonstrators are known, get stuck into their role with great enthusiasm. For the old hands, NITAT will be a refresher; for the first-time visitors, it will be an education in a different kind of soldiering.

Soldiers on patrol must remain aware of their proximity to danger

After NITAT, it is off to the Province, either for a four--and-a-half-month tour right at the sharp end on the border, or for a two-year residential tour in a region where the pressure is not quite so great. This does not mean that those on a long posting get an easy ride; it is simply that no-one could stand the physical and mental stress of the four-and-a-half-month soldier's programme for two years straight. The concentrated patrolling in danger areas, and the Quick Reaction Force duties, which mean 24 hours on standby fully kitted out, flak jackets and all, saps the strength and stamina of even the fittest and most dedicated soldier.

One cause of stress is that soldiers on patrol must remain constantly aware of their proximity to danger. A veteran of Northern Ireland roulement tours explains:

'You don't, especially in small towns that are renowned for trouble, try and walk over a manhole cover that's gone off before. You don't pick the obvious gate to climb over, you try an alternative route. If you go out for a couple of days, then sometimes — it depends on what

you've been doing — for a lot of the lads it can be quite a relief to get back inside the camp before they have to go out again in day or two.'

Then there is the sheer physical hardship of working long hours, day after day after day. The Para again:

'Within a company, you can go out on patrol for two days, come back to barracks and do sangar duty for a day, and then go straight on to maybe fatigues, and that may be a four-day cycle; then after that, after your fatigues, there's briefings again and then back out for another two days, and the cycle will just keep on for four and a half months. So it is quite hard work.'

'Nobody's interested in going to Belfast or Enniskillen for a pint'

Not only is a roulement tour hard work, but the lifestyle, paticularly in the confines of a sangar, can be very restrictive. Yet the Toms seem to manage to find ways to occupy that time which is not actually spent on stag. The Para again:

'The first time I went over there, it was a good summer and all the lads took weights with them. In the sangars — before they put roofs on them — you could sit in the forecourt and do weights, etc. You could play various games if they sent them out to you. And every couple of weeks they used to take you out of the sangar and take you to a main base and maybe give you a week off. But you were still on duty within the camp; you just weren't on duty outside the normal barracks.'

'All the times that I've been to Northern Ireland we've had a policy of nobody going out into the local area — pubs, clubs, anything else. It doesn't seem to be the done thing [in the Paras] to go out. It's just do the work, and when you need to go out on patrol, you go out. Nobody's interested in going to Belfast or Enniskillen for a pint. It isn't even thought of.'

Is the Regiment really 'Ready for Anything', as its motto claims?

This lack of freedom can pose problems for a regiment as keen on fitness as the Paras. The Toms can lift weights within the confines of a camp, but what can be done about training for the heart and lungs? In many cases, the answer has to be 'Run round the camp'. But, when it might take 50 circuits to complete three miles, this is obviously a far from ideal way to maintain the type of stamina that will carry them through a 10-miler when they get back to Aldershot, even if, on the round-the-camp runs, 'We have some of the guys hanging out with water buckets and trying to catch people, just to keep everybody smiling.'

Yet maintain fitness they must, more than any other

regiment, wherever they may be in the world. For even while they are engaged in one role — on the streets of Northern Ireland, for example — the call may come for them to assist in an Out-of-Area operation at very short notice, and the Paras must be able to cope immediately. That they have managed to do so so far is, to a large extent, a credit to their training, of which overseas acquaintance visits are as much a part as 10-milers are. But is the Regiment really 'Ready for Anything', as its motto claims? A warrant officer from 2 PARA (out of role at the time of writing) gives his verdict:

'The adaptability of this regiment sometimes even amazes me. For example, we have just sent a load of guys out to Cyprus where it is very hot at the moment, while it is not very warm here. They will go out there, and from day one they will be out running around, doing 10-milers every few days or so; really grafting and working and taking full advantage of the situation.

'Some of us went Down South, and it wasn't slowly going from normal European weather all the way down to Arctic weather: it comes on you suddenly. Yet on they go; it is irrelevant where they are. They have the gear. If they need more, they know they can get more, hopefully. Sometimes they can't, of course, but they are always prepared for that. That is what I find so astonishing about the Regiment.

'With just six hours notice, they would be ready to move'

'We could take 2 PARA now and put them in Parachute Regiment role — the ready-to-go-anywhere-parachute-anytime role. If they sent one of the other battalions out now, and it was decimated on landing or something and needed replacing straight-away, they could take 2 PARA. With just six hours notice, they would be ready to move; ready to go parachuting, loading up — obviously not getting everybody back from Cyprus [in that time], but they would already be on the way back. And they could go and do that role just as well as the two battalions that had been practising it for the last year or so. And that is what is good about this regiment.'

Left: An 'O' Group on Exercise Caltrop Force. Commanders receive their orders from their direct superiors, extract what they need, and pass it down at their own 'O' Groups.

Below: Men of 1 PARA on exercise in the USA jump from a C-141B Starlifter, the first jump from a jet for most. A C-141B can carry almost twice as many paras as a Hercules Mk3.

WEEKEND WARRIORS

On a Friday evening, men from all walks of life don the Red Beret for a weekend training as part of the TA Parachute Regiment. But why do these men give up an evening down the pub or a night with their loved ones to jump out of aeroplanes and spend two days cold, wet and knackered?

Not everyone in The Parachute Regiment is a seven-day-a-week Airborne Soldier. For besides the three regular battalions, there are also three in the Territorial Army — 4, 10 and 15 PARA. At weekends, and for one night a week and one two-week stretch every year, these part-time Paras 'train hard to fight easy'. They are men who keep up a civilian job yet, also maintain the fitness and skills of a paratrooper. The TA Para may not be a regular, but he still has the Parachute Regiment ethos, he still does 'P' Company, he still wears the Red Beret and he still jumps into battle. And all in his free time.

Like the other 'independent units' of the TA, the three Parachute Regiment TA battalions have a nucleus of Regular Army staff to run the day-to-day administration and to organise and assist in training. Companies, and often platoons, each have their own 'TA Centre' — what used to be called a 'Drill Hall'. At each company location there is a Regular Company Sergeant Major or Colour Sergeant, known as an SPSI (Senior Permanent Staff Instructor), to advise and assist the TA staff with training. There is also a QPSI (Quartermaster Permanent Staff Instructor) — a Colour Sergeant or Sergeant who is responsible for the stores held by the company. When the Company turns out, the TA staff take over some of the

A GPMG team from 15 PARA training in street fighting near Hammelberg. Note the large amount of ammunition that has been expended. Street fighting is very ammo-intensive.

functions of the PSIs: the TA CSM is responsible for the smooth running of the company, its discipline, and its weapons; the TA CQMS (Company Quartermaster Sergeant) takes over the running of the store, and keeping the men fed, watered, clothed and equipped. But at all times, the man responsible for the company as a whole is the Officer Commanding the company, known as the OC. He is an officer in the TA — sometimes a captain, but usually a major. And when the company is in the field, it is run completely by TA officers and NCOs.

The role of the PSIs is to guide and advise, to give the Territorials the benefit of their long years of experience; to teach when necessary, and to point the men in the right direction. On exercises, their job is to act like the DS (Directing Staff) on a course — standing back, observing, and then afterwards debriefing the companies and advising the officers on where their men need instruction.

The three TA battalions have centres spread the length of Britain

At battalion level, the Regular staff do not have TA counterparts to take over at drill nights and at weekends. The CO (Commanding Officer) is usually Regular, but he can sometimes be a Territorial — in which case he must take a two-year leave of absence from work. The Regimental Sergeant Major, though, is always from one of the Regular battalions, as are the adjutant and the QM (Quartermaster).

The three TA battalions have centres spread the length of Britain, so apart from in the South-West and Wales, there are few places that are very far from a Parachute Regiment TA Centre. For example, 4 PARA is based in the North-West, with its headquarters in Pudsey, Yorkshire, and companies from Lincoln to Oldham to Geordieland. The headquarters of 10 PARA is in London, but the battalion has sub-units (companies and platoons) based as far apart as Portsmouth, Southend and Aldershot. The Scottish TA battalion is 15 PARA, with its headquarters in Glasgow and companies and platoons throughout Scotland.

The numbering of the battalions may seem strange, but when the Territorial Army was reformed in 1947, it had nine battalions, numbered from 10 to 18 and forming the 16th Airborne Division. With the successive cuts in the reserve forces since then, only 10 and 15 PARA have remained in their original form, while 12 and 13 PARA have amalgamated, later joining with 17 PARA to make up a new battalion, 4 PARA.

Training takes place on 'training nights' — what used

Top: Soldiers from 10 PARA clean their weapons.
Bottom: Officers in the TA must still look after the welfare of their men, even though they may see them only once or twice a week.

to be called 'drill nights' until it was decided that the word 'drill' gave entirely the wrong idea about what the TA did of an evening. For one evening every week, bank clerks and bricklayers, security guards and electricians, students and civil servants change from civilians to soldiers. As they step out of their jeans, T-shirts, suits and dirty overalls and into their boots and 'lightweights' (green Army trousers), they become Parachute Regiment Soldiers — literally. For whenever they are in uniform, whenever they put on the Red Beret, they come under military discipline and Army law. Men who normally might shave only one day in two, and who wouldn't dream of ironing their T-shirts, turn up for TA duty with stubble removed and razor sharp creases in their lightweights.

At either 1930 or 2000 hrs, the men form up in uniform as a squad, or 'fall in', as it is termed. After a quick inspection, they get down to business, learning anything from how to fire an anti-tank rocket to how to use a radio, from how to clear an enemy-held house to how to keep their buddy alive if he has been gassed. Or there may be fitness training on the programme, or a sports night, or an eight-mile run with weighted bergens.

At 2130 or 2200 hrs, depending on the start time, everyone falls back in again to hear what training is planned for the coming week. After that, they are all free to return to their wives and girlfriends, or they can relax for a while in the bar before going home. Almost every TA Centre has a bar, but the Territorial Battalions of The Parachute Regiment are by no means drinking clubs. Anyone who only turned up for the social events would soon be discharged and chucked out.

There is no threat of discipline breaking down

But the bar does have an important part to play in the life of the Company — similar in some ways to that played by the officers' and sergeants' messes in a Regular Battalion. Most bars are mixed messes — officers, NCOs and Toms all drink together — so after 10 o'clock, the Company Commander can discuss training with his PSIs, the platoon sergeant and platoon commander can sort out their men's problems, and NCOs and officers can keep in touch with the feelings, attitudes and concerns of the Toms. The bar also allows the members of the company to mix and get to know each other, and so helps to build up the cohesion of the company. To bind people closer, it is important for them to be able to both work and relax together. And there is no threat of discipline breaking down. As one sergeant in a TA Para battalion puts it:

'You're not a civilian in the Paras. The TA Parachute Regiment is not a drinking club, it's not a boysy-boysy, "Oh, he's a mate of mine" sort of thing. It doesn't work

like that. He's a sergeant, he's a corporal, he's a lance corporal, and what he says, you do. It's military discipline, and the guys respect that. Anybody who can't take the discipline, well, we just don't want them. They don't last long anyway; they don't get through the system.'

Airborne Soldiers are tabbing to the start line for a dawn assault

But the weekends are what most men join for, for exercises in the field and training together as a company or battalion. They begin, like the training nights, with men coming back from work, grabbing a bite to eat, picking up all their kit and turning up at their company in time for the parade at 2000 hrs on Friday night. Everyone then draws their webbing, rifles and other kit from the stores. As orders for the jump and 'subsequent operations' start passing down the chain of command, the training centre becomes a hectic ant-hill of activity, with men stowing brew-kits in their webbing and stuffing their bergens with equipment, sergeants dishing out ammo and organising their men, officers receiving their orders from the company commander, and small groups of Toms huddling round their section commanders, all poring over a map.

Often, everyone packs their containers on the training night before the exercise in order to save time on the Friday night. But there is always someone who turns up

A day at the ranges. A high standard of marksmanship is an essential in the TA. To this end, all ranks must take the Annual Personal Weapon Test (APWT) each year.

on the weekend who didn't attend during the week, so everybody piles in to help, with six pairs of hands battling with the straps of the CSPEP.

By midnight at the latest, everything is ready. The company then climbs aboard a coach or truck for the drive to an RAF airfield. Almost immediately, it's heads down and catch some sleep. The journey is usually two to three hours long, and it's often the only chance to sleep that anyone will get before Saturday night, when they might catch a couple of hours — if they're lucky.

All too soon, the coaches pass through the airfield gates. The men stir and prepare to get off the coach. As all the companies start to arrive from their different locations, the battalion begins to draw and fit 'chutes. For the next two or three hours, the order of the day is checking of equipment, 'chalk parades' (sorting out which men are going to go on which aircraft and in which order), and briefings — all the tasks necessary before any parachute drop. The RAF also provide loads of tea and pies. Presumably, this is so that if you puke in the aircraft you've got something to bring up — or maybe, given the taste of the pies, it's to make *sure* you puke in the aircraft.

P-Hour, the time of the parachute drop, is usually

between five and seven in the morning. For the next 25 to 30 hours, the battalion might practise helicopter moves, river crossing (without boats), patrolling, escape and evasion, a battalion assault, fighting in built-up areas, defence, or movement as a battalion; not all on the same weekend, but it sometimes seems like it.

While their family, friends and workmates are relaxing at home, doing the Saturday shopping or watching the telly, the men of the Territorial Battalions are storming bridges, tabbing across Salisbury Plain, or flying in a helicopter. But, however hard, wet, cold or hot the weekend may be, at the back of every TA soldier's mind there is always the thought that by Sunday afternoon it will all be over, though that seems little consolation when you're fighting your way up the near-vertical slope of Pen-Y-Fan with a heavy bergen on your back.

On Sunday morning, there is the final attack. While those at home might still have five or six more hours in bed, the part-time Airborne Soldiers are tabbing to the start line for a dawn assault — dog tired, but still going. If

it is a weekend of firing live rounds (in the field, but at wooden targets), then the final attack is probably made in platoon strength and with live mortar fire in support. With live grenades being used as well, a realisation of what could happen if someone made a mistake keeps everyone wide awake despite their lack of sleep. If it's an attack with blank rounds and thunder flashes, then the opposition is often from another regiment. That is when the competitive regimental spirit comes into play, bringing out the enthusiasm in even the most tired TA Para.

At about 0900 hrs, the cry 'ENDEX' goes up and everything stops

Attacks such as these are not just a matter of running around shouting, of firing blank rounds and playing 'cowboys and indians'. They are designed to practise battle drills and battle procedure all the way up the chain of command. Usually, PSIs from both sides act as umpires, sending back sub-units that don't do an attack properly and allocating the 'casualties' they would have suffered. These 'casualties' are then not allowed to take part in the exercise for a given period of time, so each platoon and company is reduced in numbers for a while.

A GPMG gunner from 10 PARA on exercise against 'hats' in Imber Village on Salisbury Plain. Note that he stands well back from the window to avoid being spotted.

At about 0900 hrs, the cry 'ENDEX' goes up and everything stops. Both sides then unload their weapons, take off their 'fighting order', and clear up the exercise area — filling in trenches, clearing out any of the empty houses in the area that have been used, and rolling up barbed wire. Then, after brunch (which is invariably stew), the companies climb onto trucks or coaches and go their separate ways back to their training centres.

Weekends are the bread and butter of the Territorial Army Airborne Soldier

However, although the exercise is over, the weekend is not. The part-time Paras still have to clean their weapons and equipment and hand them back in to stores and armouries. The first chance they get after ENDEX, they start 'laying into' their machine guns and rifles — stripping them, pulling through their barrels, and scraping off the carbon deposits from the gas parts. And this continues on the way home, on stuffy coaches and crowded four-tonners. Forever fighting the constant battle against drifting asleep, they sometimes lose it momentarily, waking up seconds later with their rifles still across their knees but their cleaning kits scattered across the floor.

Back at the training centre, there is always something more to do on the weapons, and the fighting order, parachuting equipment, digging tools, radios, and 101 other things all have to be cleaned off and handed in. It is at this stage that the SNCOs and sergeant-majors come into their own, 'gripping' the Toms with time-honoured phrases such as: 'The sooner you get this done the sooner we can go home', and: 'It's your own time you're wasting.'

After an hour or two of hectic activity and standing in queues, it's all finished and the company is dismissed — the weekend is officially over. But not everyone goes home. Several stay for a while longer before going back to wives, girlfriends or a hot bath. Over a couple of pints — orange juice for the drivers — these die-hards discuss the weekend just gone or the training yet to come. It's a chance to wind down; to catch up a little on the relaxation they've missed on Friday and Saturday nights; or to put off seeing the wife for a little bit longer.

Weekends are the bread and butter of the Territorial Army Airborne Soldier — his chance to keep in practice with his parachuting skills, to train with his mates in the company and to learn new skills in a realistic setting. But it takes the two weeks of continuous training at camp for him to really get into the routine of living in the field, to start working as a member of a tight team with the rest of his section, and to really 'put his Army head on' — to start

A soldier from 15 PARA on exercise. At the end of the barrel of his SLR is a Blank Firing Attachment (BFA); without this, the weapon will not recock when blanks are being fired.

thinking and acting much more like a soldier and less like a civilian. After about 10 days at camp, everyone is working much better as a team, and companies and battalions are much tighter knit. Individual skills have been remembered, new ones learnt and battle drills honed. Then, just as the Paras are 'getting it together', it's time to go home to be back at work for Monday morning.

The TA Parachute battalions are earmarked to reinforce the British forces in Germany in a period of tension or war, so every other year they spend camp in Germany. At other times, it tends to be in some hilly, windswept corner of the British Isles where the rain falls horizontally, such as Sennybridge in Wales or Warcop in Cumbria.

Most TA Paras prefer camps in Germany. For one thing, it gives them a chance to beat the 'hats' in battle. Regimental spirit is strong, and the Territorial Airborne

Soldier likes to test his ability against other regiments. At weekends, it is usually the same TA battalion as enemy, but on the big exercises in BAOR (British Army Of the Rhine, or British Army Over the Road), there's a whole range of corps and regiments. And on most of these German exercises, the TA Parachute Battalions act as 'orange forces' (the 'bad' guys) — jumping behind the lines, dashing about in helicopters, or patrolling deep behind 'blue force' (the 'good' guys) lines.

This suits the mentality of the Airborne soldier, allowing him to use his initiative and cunning to the full. For he takes great pleasure in causing maximum inconvenience

Troops of 15 PARA storm Bonnland village near Hammelberg. The buildings are real, as this used to be a living village before it became part of the German school of infantry.

Men of 15 PARA at Sennybridge on their two-week annual camp. Because of their role in Germany, they are training for an NBC environment, hence the 'Noddy' (NBC) suits.

to the enemy, whoever he is. On one exercise, a small patrol grounded a whole squadron of Harriers that was hidden among trees by simply stealing the ignition 'keys', while another discovered the deployment of a regiment of anti-aircraft missiles through deception and bluff. A third captured a bridge from a platoon of sleeping Germans. As the indignant German lieutenant strongly protested that he wasn't on the same exercise, the unconcerned Toms — already reinforced by the weapons the Germans had left in their trenches — simply walked off with their mineral water as well. And when one patrol 'bounced' another bunch of soldiers, the roughly handled 'hats' cried: 'You can't do that, we're only TA!' To which the Paras gleefully replied: 'So are we', and continued to tie them up.

But camp is not just 15 days of solid training. There is usually a night and a day off — the chance to go out on the town together in a different part of the world, be that town Hamburg, Porthcawl or Appleby. Once more, exploring a strange city as a group and relaxing together after a week in the field helps to cement friendships within the company and form a stronger bond between them. Whether the local townspeople are equally happy with these invasions is open to question.

'Why do I do this, why do I come back year after year?'

Because annual camp is such a concentrated and valuable period of training, every TA soldier (not just a Para) has to attend with his battalion, or have a very good reason not to. Sometimes, men do not get extra time off work to attend, and so have to give up their precious holidays. And all of them have to give up free time at week-ends and evenings. So why do they do it?

The Regular army instructors themselves often wonder about this, and so do some of the men themselves. As one sergeant in 10 PARA puts it:

'When you're freezing cold and you're lying in an ambush or going through a river crossing at 3 o'clock in the morning up to your nuts and then your neck in freezing muddy water, you think: "What the bloody hell am I doing here?" And you know exactly what your missus is doing — she's tucked up warm in bed, and all your mates have been on the piss and are now sleeping it off.

'I have absolutely no idea why I go. Sense of achievement, challenge — probably all that, but I can't put my finger on it. I don't know why.'

Or as one Tom puts it: 'They sit there kicking themselves, saying: "Why do I do this, why do I come back year after year?", and it's a difficult question to answer.'

But, while the men themselves might not know why they keep coming back, a PSI who spent two years with a TA company believes the answer can be found by analysing what he identifies as three different types of part-time Para: those who are only in the TA Parachute Regiment because it is 'this year's hobby', and therefore soon leave; those who are in it simply because they enjoy it, and will leave when they stop enjoying it; and those for whom it is a commitment, one that they will fulfil, no matter what. Of course, any or all of these three 'types' can apply to an individual TA Para during his career. A lot of them start off seeing the TA as a short-term thing — this year's hobby — but their view gradually alters as they go away on more and more weekends with their units, and before long, they are in one of the other categories.

As the runs get longer, the weight gets heavier and the pace gets quicker

Also, even many of the 'this year's hobby' variety join for the very real challenge of getting into The Parachute Regiment, albeit one of the Territorial battalions. For the TA Paras must do Pre-Parachute Selection, though in a slightly different form to the Regulars. As one Tom puts it:

'It was a challenge. I have always been reasonably fit, so it was more a mental thing rather than physical; I quite enjoyed the experience.'

A recruit entering a TA Parachute battalion does the Territorial 'P' Company about three months after he first walked through the door of the training centre. In that time, he will have spent his weekends and training nights learning weapon handling, drill and map reading. This is basically what his regular counterpart does at Depot, but because the TA has (probably) got a full-time civilian job as well, he gets less time to practice. And he must also work hard at his fitness. After his day's work, he has to rush down to the training centre, put 16kg on his back and then push himself to the limit and beyond, assisted by TA instructors. For this reason, each training night tends to act in itself as a sort of selection period, sorting out the committed from the diletante. As the runs get longer, the weight gets heavier and the pace gets quicker, and every time the recruits parade, their numbers diminish.

Perhaps 10 out of the original 30 will make it through to the end

At the end of those first three months, out of perhaps 30 that walked through the training centre doors at the beginning, less than half remain. These die-hards will now go on to 'recruit camp' at Depot. Then, after two weeks of intense physical and mental pressure, of more weapons training, NBC — Nuclear, Biological, Chemical (warfare) — drills, a short exercise in the field and fitness work, comes 'P' Company. This is slightly different to the Regular Army "P" Company, as there is no Exercise 'Steel Bayonet' — the Welsh phase. But the Trainasium causes the same fear and the 10-miler the same pain — although for the TAs there is a straight pass or fail time of two hours. And there is still a Stretcher Race, run through the soft sand and deep ruts of a tank-testing course; still the same Log Race over the same course with the same logs; still the same Assault Course, Steeplechase and Milling.

Perhaps 10 out of the original 30 will make it through to the end and receive their Red Berets on the final Sunday. They then return to their companies and, when they next get two weeks off work, go to Brize Norton for the TA Basic Parachuting course. Once again, because a TA soldier often has a civilian job to hold down, time is limited, and so what the Regular learns over four weeks, the part-time Para has to absorb in only two. But that makes no difference where the actual jumping is concerned: standing at the edge of the balloon cage is the same, whether you've been there for two weeks or four. There is, however, one less jump on the TA course — the night jump.

It is at this stage that those who joined merely in order to get the beret and the wings stop turning up — unless they have become committed. As one Tom puts it:

'I wasn't too interested in the Regular Army at the time. Initially, I only joined the TA to learn to parachute, and I didn't know too much about the forces in general. I didn't know anything about "P" Company, or what you had to do before you even got to Brize Norton.'

Yet he has stayed in because he finds being a part-time Para challenging and rewarding, and sees it as: 'a sort of test of character, of your own self-reliance in situations that you're not normally in during the week.

'Sometimes, you think: "Why am I doing this?" Most of

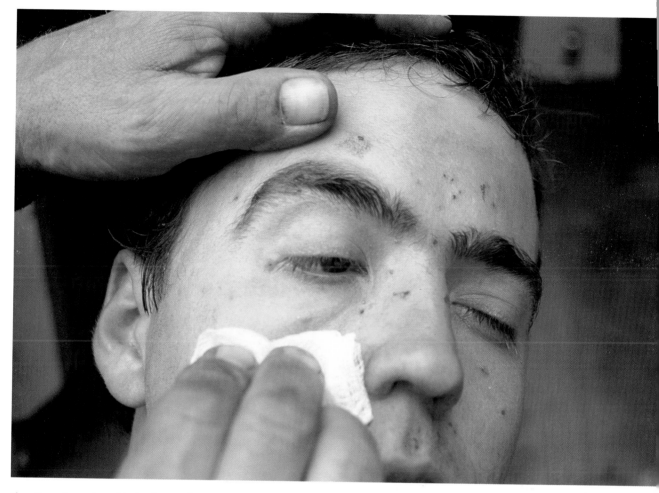

the time there is a kind of apprehension about something, like when everybody is in the aircraft before a lob [jump]. But generally, either during it [the jump] or just after, you think: "That was worthwhile", or: "That wasn't too bad, I quite enjoyed that".'

'I'm a bit masochistic, I suppose. I like hardship and a test of strength'

To want to do this at weekends after a working week takes the sort of character who wants more than just the creature comforts of today's society. The Tom again:

'I guess I don't particularly like evenings with my feet up, I'm not that type of person. I'm a bit masochistic, I suppose. I like hardship and a test of strength; you can't get that by sitting in front of the television.'

A TA Tom dashes from a doorway while his mate provides covering fire. Training for this sort of fire and manoeuvre is vital in built-up areas, where danger lurks at every window.

The effects of a blank round fired negligently into a face from close range. This soldier was lucky that the 'wadding', the material packed into the cartridge, did not take his eye out.

It certainly seems to be the case that the harder the weekend, the more most TA Paras enjoy it. Not at the time, maybe, but afterwards, when they can enjoy a large sense of achievement.

Some of those TA paras who are 'in it because they enjoy it' will have already had a taste of soldiering during their time in the Army Cadet Force or another TA unit, and have subsequently 'caught the bug'. They have found that they enjoy infantry work, and they join The Parachute Regiment because: 'It's recognised as the finest infantry regiment, and that goes for the TA as well as the Regular Army', as one TA Para puts it. Such is their pride in the Regiment, and their desire to be a part of 'the best', that many part-time Paras spend hours just travelling to and from drill nights and weekends, even though there may be some other TA unit within walking distance of their home.

Men of 15 PARA take it easy as they wait to emplane for a paradrop onto the Sennybridge training area in Wales. They are wearing life vests in case they land in the sea.

So why don't such people join the Regular Army? A Tom gives his reasons:

'I decided to join the TA because the commitment is less. Also, you have the best of both worlds, in the sense that with the TA you can do the sort of activities that you would do if you were in the Regular Army, but you don't have to go through all that stuff that you have to do in the Regular Army from day to day [such as guard duties].'

Many like the sense of freedom they get from being in the TA, the freedom of knowing that they are there because they want to be there and, if they no longer like it, they can leave. In the view of one TA Para:

'You see, it's easy for us not to turn up. If you could write on a piece of paper all the reasons why you like the Army, you'd find you can get those from the TA. If you wrote down the reasons why you *don't* want to be in the Army — well, the Regulars can keep those.'

'There is a guy in this company who was in 2 PARA for three years, and in three years he only went to Northern Ireland. Since joining the TA three years ago, he has been to Canada, America, Gibraltar, he has done an unarmed combat course, he has gone to Germany twice, and he has now gone to Germany again for a wings course. He has never done so many courses; he never got as much out of the Army as he has from the TA.'

There are many courses and attachments a TA Para can go on if he has the free time. He can join a Regular Parachute battalion for a six- to 18-month period on what is known as an 'S', or 'Special' type engagement; he can do an NCO's course at Brecon, or a training course for one of the specialist platoons — Assault Pioneers, MILAN, Signals, Mortars; and he can go on exercise to Cyprus, Canada or Germany, either with one of the other Para battalions, or with another regiment entirely.

And for those who do go away with one of the Regular Parachute battalions, there is the family spirit of the Regiment, the bond that exists between those men who have earned the Red Beret. In the words of one Tom

from a Territorial battalion who went on attachment to 3 PARA in Cyprus: 'I fitted into a Regular company just like that, no problems at all.' In his view, at the level of the private soldier: 'There isn't a lot of difference. When we are away on a weekend, basically we are the same.' (While this may be true at the personal level, a TA battalion cannot expect to as 'ready for anything' as a Regular one — it simply doesn't have the time to train.) When that same Tom went to Cyprus, however, there were a few initial difficulties with some of the Regulars:

'Territorials could be classed as much keener than Regular soldiers'

'At first they said: "Bloody TA rubbish", and all that crap. But then we did a few runs — just seven miles or something — and the TA blokes were up front all the way, and there was no drop out. In fact, it was a *Regular* who dropped out; *we* had all got fit to go there. After that, when we had proved we could do what they do, there was no problem, they were alright.'

Trying to catch a few minutes sleep, men of 15 PARA doze on the C-130 during the flight to the DZ. Their containers are in the foreground, with the harness hooks clearly visible.

He also found, however, that: 'The Regulars never want to do the exercise, never want to do the parachuting or the shooting. They never want to do it, but all the TA blokes there wanted to do everything.'

When you do something full-time it is often difficult to maintain the enthusiasm of somebody who does it as a break from their normal job. And the enthusiasm of the TA Para is remarkable, a tremendous asset to any commander, and one which he can not afford to waste. As one Regular warrant officer puts it:

'Territorials could be classed as much keener than the Regular soldiers. Once you sign on the dotted line and are a Regular soldier, you don't get no choice in the matter. The volunteers have always had a choice. I think the Parachute Regiment Territorials leave the whole of the rest of the Army [both regular and TA] standing from the point of view of enthusiasm. I have worked [with] and

marked and graded other Regiments' TA battalions, and they are not as enthusiastic as ours.'

Many of those that stay in the TA after they have got their wings and beret do so out of a strong desire to be better soldiers. They find, however, that it is difficult for them to satisfy their thirst for knowledge or improve their skills on just weekends and training nights. As one part-time Para puts it: 'You want to give more time because you never feel you are doing enough, so it is always best to try and attend when you can.' Another, asked if he would ever think of giving up the TA, answers: 'No, there's too much to know.'

'No matter what's on, I still turn up. It's one of my loves of my life now'

Many part-time Paras, dissatisfied with the limited opportunities of just weekends and training nights, leave the TA and join one of the Regular Battalions. Others, who would like to make the Regular Army a permanent career but can't — either because they are not prepared to suffer a cut in salary, or because of family ties, or whatever — remain in the TA. These are the committed and determined ones, the TA Airborne Soldiers who turn up regardless of whether the weekend involves jumping into Germany or painting 4-ton trucks. They do enjoy soldiering, but it is more than that. As one TA lance corporal who has been in 5 years puts it:

'I just come along anyway. No matter what's on, I still turn up. It's one of my loves of my life now, so I don't need any excuse to turn up.'

Although this holds true throughout the rank structure, such TA Paratroopers are often NCOs and officers, responsible for planning training or running the unit. This in itself means that they must be prepared to put in far more time than the average Tom. In the view of one Sergeant who has spent nine years in a TA Parachute Battalion:

'The blokes that stay in the TA the longest are the blokes that stay at the bar the longest and the latest. They are the guys that are the corner-stone of the TA, the foundations of a good TA company. The blokes who have got all the ideas about why they joined — "I want to jump out of airplanes", and "It's a challenge" and all that old rhubarb — they disappear after six or eight months, or a year, maximum'.

The TA as a whole, not just the Parachute Regiment, has a high turnover of personnel — about 30 per cent a year. In a TA company, there is a 'hard core' of 15 to 20 officers and men who make the company work. The

A GPMG gunner moves off to provide covering fire. Obstacles are set up to add realism: coiled barbed wire can be seen in the background; there are also dummy minefields.

A far cry from an executive lunch. A TA corporal eats from an issue mess tin. The 1944 pattern water bottle in the foreground keeps water cooler than the 1958 version.

other 40 to 60 men do not turn up as frequently, and so contribute less. No matter how good a man is, he's not much use to the company unless he attends.

The hard core who are there every time and are the last to leave do not see the Parachute Regiment TA as only a drinking club — weekends are far too hard to do that — but they do feel a strong sense of belonging to their unit, a strong sense of the company and battalion and Regimental spirit. They turn up every time because they don't want to let their mates down, mates who have tabbed with them on hard exercises, who have been just as cold, wet and hungry when huddling in an adjoining trench. For men such as these, the TA Parachute Regiment becomes a vital part of their life.

Yet even the most committed part-time Para still has a life outside the TA that he must attend to. He has to juggle his work, his personal or domestic life, and the TA. Sometimes, he needs to emphasise one of these commitments more than the other two. The outlook of his workmates is often totally different, and leave from employers is not always forthcoming, as one SNCO describes:

'They all think I'm mad. They're all too busy at weekends getting drunk, partying, and having a good time. They don't think along the same sort of lines that I do. My boss laughs about it and all that, but he won't give me any bloody time off.'

Keeping fit can also be a problem, as a Sergeant describes: 'I find it very difficult at present, because of the hours I work and everything, but I manage to struggle along and keep as fit as I can. It is awkward — just the time factor, really.'

Finances can also be a hindrance, since the TA pay is so much lower than some Paras' wages. Also, with the scale of wages in some civilian jobs, since a man can earn only £35 with the TA over a weekend there is a considerable disincentive to turn up for training — particularly if he has a family to support. As one NCO puts it:

'I mean, the Army money is a joke compared to what I make in civvy street. If the mortgage rates go up any more, I may have to cut down [my TA activities] a bit and work weekends.'

There will always be men who want something different

Another pressure on the home front comes from wives and girlfriends. Some TA Paras are lucky, as one explains: 'She can't understand why I do it, but she doesn't mind. She understands that I need that little bit of space.' But most have girlfriends who are not so accommodating, as one describes: 'The girlfriend thinks it's a pain in the arse, because she can't go out on Saturday night.'

It is because of these competing pressures that the TA Para requires excellent man management, both from those that plan his training and those that organise him directly. As one part-time Tom puts it:

'The last few months we have had like a week between each weekend, and that's been OK. But this month coming up I'll be away for two weekends in a row. It's that sort of thing which isn't a good idea. And also, when you have bank holidays — we have had two this month and we have had exercises on both of them. The first one there was a very poor turn-out because the TA, if they get a long weekend off they will try and make the most of it with their girlfriends or family or whatever.'

If a Regular Tom gets 'hacked off', he doesn't sign on again when his three or five years are up. If a TA Paratrooper is 'fed up', he just stops turning up. So it is important to ensure that he is organised and administered smoothly and efficiently. As one part-time Para puts it:

A 15 PARA soldier looks to his feet. Foot hygiene is very important in the field. A TA weekend is too short to feel its effects, but a two-week camp is another story.

ENDEX at Hammelberg and end of weekend. TA Paras leave for the drill hall and 'civvy street' — for another week.

'The worst part of the weekend is getting out of your house on Friday night and getting here and getting to the training area. But once you're in the training area, it's alright.'

Although he makes a commitment to turn up regularly when he joins his battalion, the part-time Para is still a volunteer. If an interesting training schedule is organised, he will actually want to turn up, as one TA Tom describes:

'Over recent months, the training programmes have got a lot more varied and interesting, and so you actually want to come in and learn something new and do something.'

But despite the pressure from the civilian side of their lives, the TA Paratroopers continue to give up their free time to go cold, wet and hungry while learning how to be more professional soldiers, and continue to risk serious injury making regular parachute jumps. For there will always be men who want something different, something more than an everyday, nine-to-five, down-the-pub-at-weekends existence. As one part-time Tom sums it up:

'You finish work on a Friday, get into your kit, and go away for a weekend. You jump in, blow everybody up, kill everyone, and then you come back to work on Monday and you're listening to people saying how good their roses are coming on.'

THE AIRBORNE BROTHERHOOD

There is a common bond that links all paratroopers, regardless of their nationality. It was forged in the shared hardship and danger of joint operations, and it still holds good today, in the shared hardship and danger of modern training. Since the formation of The Parachute Regiment, the almost universal mark of membership of this 'Airborne Brotherhood' has been the Red Beret — and this has come to symbolise the traditional Airborne qualities.

When the Parachute Training School was set up at Ringway Airport in Manchester in 1940 to train the first British Paras, Airborne forces had already been in existence elsewhere for more than a decade. The first para-trained unit, a force of company size, was unveiled by the Italians in 1928. Two years later, the Soviet Union formed a parachute battalion, and in 1937, the first French para unit was created. But in general, World War II was to be the launching pad for Airborne forces, and it was the success of another pioneer parachuting army that started the ball rolling.

In April 1940, Germany unleashed her paratroop force, the *Fallschirmjaeger,* on Norway and then, in May, on the Netherlands. The success of these operations convinced certain key figures in the British leadership, notably Winston Churchill, of the potential of the para-

1 PARA waiting to board USAF C-141 Starlifters for the jump into Exercise 'Caltrop Force' in California, March 1989.

trooper as a serious instrument of war. Indeed, Churchill was so impressed that he called for the creation of a 5000-man parachute contingent. Training began.

Once established, the British Airborne Forces were influential in the development of parachute units in other countries because of Britain's links with the Commonwealth and the free forces of the occupied European nations. Within a year, an Indian parachute battalion had been approved, and in 1942, the Belgian paras started training at Ringway and were incorporated into the British Paras in 1943. But not all Commonwealth countries came to Britain for Airborne training.

The Red Beret became the universal symbol of the Airborne Soldier

The Canadian Airborne Forces came into being in 1942 with the formation of the Canadian Parachute Battalion. Although it was later to serve in Europe with the British 6th Airborne Division, the battalion underwent its para training with the US Airborne Forces, which themselves had been created within a month of Britain's training beginning at Ringway Airport. Although they were formed entirely independently of the British Paras and formulated

Paras lined up in front of converted Whitley bombers at Ringway Airport for a training jump during WWII. The Whitley could drop 10 men, the Hercules Mk 3 can drop 90.

their own training programme, they still chose to wear the Red Beret, as did the Belgian, Indian and Canadian paras.

The Red Beret was destined to become the almost universal symbol of the Airborne Soldier. But this is only the outward sign of a special bond that developed between paras of the various armies as a result of combined operations during World War II. Among the most famous of these were the D-Day operations of June 1944, and Operation Market Garden later the same year.

They had proved themselves to be gutsy, trouble-shooting troops

In the first of these, the British 6th Airborne Division, which included the 1st Canadian Parachute Battalion, jumped on one flank of the beachhead, while the US 82nd and 101st Airborne Divisions jumped on the other, a prelude to the Allied assault on Normandy. In the second, the same American formations dropped on Eindhoven, Grave and Nijmegen, while the British jumped at Arnhem.

In both operations, the parachute and airlanding forces were used as spearhead troops, sent in to secure key objectives ahead of the main thrust. Lightly armed because of the limitations of what could be delivered by air, they constantly came up against stronger and more heavily equipped opposition and had to go it alone until relieved.

The feats of arms achieved by the Airborne forces in these and other operations led to a mystique growing up

British Paras about to jump through the hole in the floor of a Whitley during WWII. Not until the RAF adopted the US C-47 Dakota did they have the luxury of jumping through a door.

around them. The role of spearhead, combined with jumping into battle or being landed by glider, was highly dangerous, and they had proved themselves to be gutsy, trouble-shooting troops, led by officers of a like mind. A mutual respect grew up between the various nationalities thrust together in adversity, a respect felt because men recognised like attitudes, like abilities and like experience. It was this similarity of character and the dangers that all faced which laid the foundation for a kind of unofficial Airborne club — the Airborne Brotherhood.

But membership of the Airborne Brotherhood was not limited to Allied paras and airlanding forces; this mutual respect also extended to German Airborne troops. The German paras were highly regarded as fighters among the British Airborne Forces who had encountered them in North Africa, Italy and Sicily, and during the battle for Arnhem. It was the heavily depleted German 1st Parachute Division which held Monte Cassino against a combined Allied force in early 1944. It is ironic that the very troops that acted as such a catalyst to the formation

of Airborne forces in Britain and the USA were permanently grounded within a year of taking blitzkrieg to the Netherlands. Though ultimately successful, the German invasion of Crete — Operation Merkur — was so expensive in terms of human lives that the German paras were never used in the Airborne role again, and reverted to line infantry. Nevertheless, they had been trained as a crack force, and a crack force they remained.

The Airborne Brotherhood is as strong today as it was during World War II

The Airborne forces did not vanish with the reduction of armies to peacetime levels after the war. Rather, as most conflicts tend to be of a localised nature and of short duration, the Airborne forces have been most useful as the spearhead of their respective armies, and have seen more action than most. Parachute assaults are now rare, but this has not stopped governments from calling on their Airborne forces first, using them as crack infantry outfits. The Israeli paras were used like this in the more recent rounds of the Arab-Israeli conflict, as was The Parachute Regiment itself in the Falklands. Combined drops no longer take place, yet the Airborne Brotherhood is as strong

Above: Men of 1 PARA at Arnhem, Holland, September 1944.
Left: *Fallschirmjaeger* manning an MG42 at Monte Cassino.
Though fighting for totally different causes, British and
German paras respected each others' battlefield prowess.

World War II set the standard for what could be expected of an Airborne Soldier, and that tradition has been carried on, with the result that the title 'Airborne' has become synonymous with élite. The standard was, and still is, demanded by the trouble-shooting role which sets them apart. This role in turn demands harsh and dangerous training to bring out the classic Airborne qualities,, and to instil the universal Airborne outlook, to which other paras can relate. This training is also important in that it serves as a test of character, one that has taken the place of regular parachute operations in forging a bond between Airborne officers and men through a common experience. In other words, if a soldier is Airborne, he must be all right.

An insight into how important training is in conferring 'Brotherhood' status is given by the fact that British Paras do not look on corps troops in 5 Airborne Brigade as being in the Brotherhood unless they have passed 'P' Company. Giving a soldier a Red Beret and calling him

today as it was during World War II. A Para NCO explains:

'There is an affinity between Airborne troops. If you were in a battle with, say, our infantry, you would have more affinity with the German paras than you would have with the Royal Welshers, or whatever.'

'Airborne' does not magically imbue him with all the qualities that an Airborne Soldier must have.

Nowadays, contact is maintained between the various Airborne forces, not through combined actions, but through joint exercises, exchange postings, and regimental visits. The Paras frequently go abroad to see their Commonwealth and foreign counterparts: in battalion or company strength for joint training exercises, or as small teams in order to take part in parachuting competitions, or as individuals on exchange postings to, for example, the United States. In return, the Paras extend their hospitality to foreign paras, and regularly have officers of overseas Airborne forces seconded to one of their battalions.

Apart from fostering closer relations between the various outfits ('We [the Paras] had a good time with the Canadians out in Edmonton. They are good lads.'), these contacts allow the different Airborne forces a glimpse of how the others train. During regimental visits, it is almost customary for the visiting troops to take part in a number of drops with the home team, and be presented with that nation's wings afterwards.

But if there is an affinity between Airborne Soldiers, there is also some rivalry, with a good dose of national pride thrown in. The Paras may feel that they have more in common with some other Airborne forces than they do with the rest of their own Army, but that does not stop them believing that they are better than any other Airborne force. And not only in combat; they believe that their training is harder and their Toms fitter than anyone else's, and when comparing Airborne forces, training and fitness are often used as yardsticks. All Airborne training is tough — almost murderous, in fact, compared to practically any other branch of the services — and all Airborne Soldiers are extremely fit by normal standards. Nevertheless, the Paras judge by *their* standards, and if shortcomings in others are thought to exist, then they are pointed out.

One thing the British Paras cannot comprehend is the custom prevalent in certain branches of the Brotherhood of singing while running. A Para explains:

'The French paras are like the Americans — loads of show and loads of bloody singing. I say if you get the bastards singing, you aren't working hard enough. They go out, they carry the flag or the pennant or whatever they want, off they go and they all start singing their heads off, and when they come in they're *still* singing. We went for a four-mile run. The French set off a good quarter of a mile in front of us. They were away; we set off five, six, seven minutes after them, and we came in about 10 minutes before them. That's what it was like. We were knackered, but we just flew past these blokes and they went, "What the f—'s going on here?" We whipped past, into camp, and we were getting showered before they came in. And *that's* just training.'

But the greatest links are with the German paras, as an NCO puts it:

'We found the Germans on about the same par as ourselves. Especially when they come over to England, they always seem to like going to the balloon and spending a day up there, completing as many jumps as they can. And out in the field they seem to work well, also.'

On at least one encounter, though, they did not seem to be as fit as the British, as one Para NCO describes:

'Ours are all pretty fit boys. For example, the other day we had the German paras running with us. There were only three of them out of 20 that were conscripts, and we put them on a run with our guys. Well, apart from the odd one or two, they were well back, completely out of it.'

The Airborne Brotherhood has survived undiminished, but what of the Airborne forces themselves? In almost all cases they are much reduced in size, due in part to reduced manning levels in peacetime, and in part to the arrival of the helicopter as a convenient form of military transport; many Airborne troops these days would go to war in choppers, not by parachute. On top of this, the role of Airborne forces has undergone much re-evaluation since the war. Each nation has developed a niche for its Airborne forces in keeping with its national, international and, where applicable, global responsibilities.

The spearhead of the Airborne Corps is the 82nd Airborne Division

Where Britain has an Airborne brigade, the US Airborne Forces consist of a far larger formation. The US XVIII Airborne Corps contains one Airborne division, the 82nd, and one heliborne division, the 101st Airborne (Air Assault) Division, along with a mechanised infantry division, an armoured brigade, an artillery brigade, and an anti-tank air cavalry brigade. A Special Forces group and a Rangers infantry unit complete the ORBAT (ORder of BATtle).

The spearhead of the Airborne Corps is the 82nd Airborne Division (the 'All American'), the direct descendant of the division of the same name which fought in World War II. It is a fully parachute-capable formation, its soldiers wear the Red Beret (although this practice was interrupted in the years 1978-80), and it is the centrepiece of the US Rapid Deployment Force. In other words, it has an Out-of-Area role similar to that of 5 Airborne Brigade, but without its 'home defence' role.

With a total complement of 15-16,000, the 82nd is around three times the size of the British Airborne formation. It is organised in three parachute brigades plus artillery, support arms, and services. However, it is not only the size of the Airborne formation that matters, but also the aircraft to get it to where it is needed. The 82nd can be transported around the world by the 544 C-130

Hercules, 250 C-141 Starlifter, and 97 C-5 Galaxy aircraft of the United States Air Force. The advantage to the 82nd of having such an airfleet is not only that it can deliver men, stores and equipment in enormous quantities, but also that it can carry large and heavy equipment. In a parachute insertion though, the 82nd would have to rely initially on equipment which can be air-dropped, ruling out the heavier guns and armoured vehicles.

The 'All American' is, therefore, a lightly equipped division, with artillery support provided by 105mm towed guns and air-droppable armour in the shape of M551 Sheridan light tanks fitted with a 152mm combined gun and launcher for Shillelagh anti-tank missiles. The armoured contingent is quite small, however, for a single battalion of 54 M551s supports the whole of the 82nd Airborne Division, whereas 5 Airborne Brigade has a bat-

Left: A WW II *Fallschirmjaeger* during the battle for Anzio, Feb 1944. Behind him is a British prisoner. German paras were part of the Luftwaffe, and many were diehard Nazis. Below: Suda Bay, Crete, May 1941. British and German paras sing the same song of the "paratroopers' graveyard".

talion-sized armoured regiment — with 32 Scorpion light tanks and 30 Fox armoured cars — to itself.

This shortfall in tanks leaves a gap in two areas where armour is traditionally employed — reconnaissance, and anti-tank warfare. However, although the 82nd lacks ground vehicles, it makes up for it in helicopters: OH-58 Kiowas handle the recce, and TOW-mounting AH-1S Huey Cobras supplement the M551s in taking care of the latter problem. But Hueys have nowhere near the range of the airdrop aircraft, so would probably have to be carried in by Galaxies after the paras had secured an airhead.

The home of the US Airborne Forces is at Fort Bragg in North Carolina. This is a truly vast military complex, encompassing the headquarters and barracks of both the 82nd Airborne Division and the XVIII Airborne Corps. It has its own military training areas, and military airfields. US para commanders at Fort Bragg have all the aircraft required for a drop at their immediate disposal, and can therefore arrange for descents to take place at very short notice, rather than having to go through the long-winded British procedure of having to order aircraft and 'chutes months in advance. Indeed, there is a story of a group of

Left: Men of the US 101st Airborne Div abseiling from a Huey. The 'Screaming Eagles' was a parachute division in WWII, and still has a high proportion of para-trained troops. Above: An M60 machine gun team of the 101st on exercise.

British Paras visiting the centre who expressed a passing interest in trying out the US military parachute. The US officer accompanying them ordered up an aircraft, and in no time at all they were airborne over the local DZ.

The US Airborne training school is at Fort Benning, Georgia. Here, the British Para is confronted by scenes and methods quite different to those he is used to at Aldershot and Brize Norton. For example, parachute training at Fort Benning is carried out, not in seven-man 'sticks' with their own PJI, but en masse, and with one instructor lecturing and demonstrating to a vast throng of students via a PA system. And each instructor takes a different lesson, so there is no personal contact as there is at Brize. Training with the paras themselves will be parachute packers, since in the US Forces all packers are parachute-trained, and may be called upon to jump — an extra incentive to do their job properly. In addition to the

school at Fort Benning, the US Airborne Forces have a parachute training school at Augsburg in Germany, where the first German paratroopers were trained after the Federal German Army was formed in 1956. These became the first instructors at the Airborne and Air Transport School at Schongau when the Germans took it over in early 1958.

While the US and British Airborne Forces are volunteers, West Germany still has a system of conscription, and many recruits into their paras (*Fallschirmjaeger)* are national servicemen, which means there is less continuity than in a purely professional outfit. Candidates for the German paras undergo a selection programme immediately they are called up, and parachute training for those who are accepted comes after three months of standard infantry basic training. The German wings course lasts four weeks, with the five jumps required to qualify all being taken in the final week.

The *Bundeswehr* has no Out-of-Area responsibilities, and so the German Airborne Forces (consisting of three brigades, which together make up the 1st Airborne Division) are geared purely to fighting war on NATO's

Central Front — doing battle in their own country, in fact. Their role is anti-armour warfare (although there is a contingency for operations in enemy-held territory), and they are organised, armed and trained specifically to carry out this task. Although all the battalion is parachute trained, only two of its four combat companies are in the parachute role. These two *Fallschirmjaeger* (Airborne infantry) companies could go in as an advance force, dropping into battle from C-160 Transall aircraft (a twin-engined equivalent of the Hercules). The other two (*Fallschirmpanzerabwehr* — airborne anti-tank) companies follow in German-built CH-53 helicopters with Kraka load carriers.

The Kraka, or Faun Kraftkarren, is a very basic, light, jeep-like vehicle, rather like the British 'Supacat'. It was designed specifically for the Airborne role and can be literally folded in half; one of the 85 C-160 Transalls can carry 16 Krakas, and one of the 105 CH-53s, five. The Krakas themselves carry the heavy TOW and MILAN anti-tank missiles and 20mm anti-aircraft guns of the *Fallschirmpanzerabwehr* companies, in contrast to the British who have to hump their MILANs around on their backs. In time, the Kraka will be replaced by the Wiesel light-armoured weapons-carrier, another specially developed Airborne vehicle.

The Soviet parachute capability is on a different scale entirely

Besides receiving new equipment, the German Airborne formations are also being reorganised as part of the 'Army Structure 2000'. Instead of an Airborne division, with one of its three brigades allocated to each of the German corps, there will be two Airmobile divisions, both comprising an Airborne brigade, an anti-tank helicopter brigade, and two helicopter regiments.

If the *Fallschirmjaeger* were ever to go into action, they could well be up against the men who wear the blue beret and striped sailor's shirt of the Soviet paras. That they don't wear the Red Beret of the western branch of the Airborne Brotherhood is an indication of their totally different roots and separate development. If the US Airborne Forces dwarf Britain's 5 Airborne Brigade, the Soviet parachute capability is on a different scale entirely. The VDV (*Vozdushno-Desantnyye Voyska* — Airborne Forces) is over 100,000 strong, with seven parachute divisions, 15 independent brigades, at least one independent regiment and 30 independent battalions. (A single Soviet Airborne division has about 6500 officers and men, and as such is just bigger than 5 Airborne Brigade, but less

than half the size of the US 82nd Airborne Division.) The major role of the Soviet paras is the traditional one of a spearhead force that would parachute or airland into enemy-held territory — in the event of a conflict with NATO this would mean into western Europe — paving the way for the main ground attack.

In December 1979, the Soviets used their Airborne Forces in just this way, airlanding the 105th Guards Airborne Division at Kabul Airport, and two other regiments at Bagram airbase, as a spearhead to their intervention in Afghanistan. As this operation took place outside the Warsaw Pact-NATO zone of direct conflict, it might be seen as a type of Out-of-Area operation. But the very fact that a ground link-up was planned makes it different from the Airborne operations envisaged by 5 Airborne Brigade, most of which would have to be independent of conventional forces. That is not to say that Soviet Airborne Forces cannot mount self-contained operations; they can, and on a divisional scale.

In fact, the Soviet Airborne were the most successful of the Russian infantry deployed to Afghanistan. Whereas the motor rifle troops were initially unable to adapt to a type of warfare for which they had not been directly trained, the Airborne straight-away proved themselves to be much more flexible. They were prepared to go into the hills after the Mujahedin on foot, rather than trying to fight in the style of a conventional conflict in Europe, an approach which was inevitably doomed to failure.

While the western Airborne forces have to walk once they hit the ground — bar some heavy weapons' crews in their open Krakas and Land Rovers — the Soviets *ride* into battle once they have landed. And in purpose-built AFVs as well. For each Airborne battalion (nine of which, organised in three regiments, make up a single division) is equipped with 30 BMD-1s (*Bronevaya Maschina Desantnaya*). Each of these air-droppable, armoured infantry fighting vehicles is armed with a 73mm or 30mm gun, an AT-3 Sagger or AT-4 Spigot anti-tank missile, and three 7.62mm machine guns. In addition, it can carry six paras. There is also a 120mm self-propelled gun version, the 2S9, and a turretless command variant, the BMD M1979 — of which there are a further five in the battalion, and more at regimental and divisional level. When they were first developed the Soviets, tried dropping the vehicles with the crews *inside*. They have since given up on this idea as none of the 'volunteers' survived.

In addition to the BMDs, special air-droppable, armoured 85mm ASU-85 (*Aviadesantnaya Samakhodnaia Ustanovka*) self-propelled assault guns have been developed for the Soviet Airborne Forces. One battalion of 31 ASU-85s serves each Airborne division. With 384 armoured vehicles, a Soviet Airborne division is a powerful mechanised force, but it is still no match for a NATO armoured division. Even the

Left: C/Sgt Ted Dalton, 10 PARA, adjusting the 'chute for a US para prior to a balloon jump on Hankley Common. Following Pages: Paras of the US 82nd jumping on exercise.

frontal armour on the Warsaw Pact's Airborne AFVs is capable of stopping only a 12.7mm machine-gun bullet, while none of their weapons would even dent the latest MBT.

Like the US and Israeli paras, the French Army recruits women

Although the Soviets have enormous Airborne capacity in terms of manpower and equipment, they are limited in how much of it they can deploy at any one time. This is because of the enormous number of aircraft sorties required to move a mechanised Airborne division. Even though the Soviet Military Transport Aviation has some 2000 aircraft, it can only cope with moving three Airborne divisions over 480km at once. Over 1610km, it would only be one and a half divisions, and when a BMD-equipped regimental group takes over 200 An-12 sorties to airdrop, it is easy to see why. (The An-12 Cub is the Soviet equivalent of the Hercules.) The resources of Aeroflot could also be used, but most of their 1800 aircraft cannot drop paratroopers. But the Soviets are not the only ones with an airlift problem. It takes over 220 Hercules sorties to move a heavily equipped, full-strength 5 Airborne Brigade; the RAF has 60.

The French paras, as part of France's Rapid Action Force (FAR), have two roles: to act as a highly mobile anti-tank screen like the Germans, and as Out-of-Area trouble-shooters like 5 Airborne Brigade. Though in recent years the latter obligation has taken them to Chad, Lebanon and Zaire, their primary role is to act as a rapid reinforcement in West Germnay should a war break out on NATO's Central Front.

The Airborne formation of today's French Army is the 13,000 strong 11th Parachute Division. This includes six infantry battalions, five from the regular French Army and one, the legendary 2 REP, from the French Foreign Legion. It was this latter unit which carried out the Airborne assault on Kolwezi in 1978. Each company in this crack battalion is not only parachute-capable, but is also trained in a specialist form of warfare, be it sabotage, mountain warfare or counter-terrorism. The 2 REP also has a special class of soldiers known as assault paratroopers, who are the élite of this élite unit. Such is the mystique of the Legion that, according to one British Para who met them:

Below: A trainee German *Fallschirmjaeger* about to jump from the outdoor exit trainer at Schongau, Bavaria.
Right: German Krakas armed with 20mm automatic cannon.

'The civilians wouldn't go near those blokes, because they were legionnaires.'

The French paras have, in the finest tradition of Airborne forces, a crippling training programme. On successful completion of this, the Army paras receive a Red Beret; the 2 REP, who train at a separate establishment, wear the green beret of the Legion.

Like the US and Israeli paras, the French Army recruits women and, in common with Germany, they have conscripts in their ranks. These, should they volunteer, can be sent on Out-of-Area operations, but the usual practice in emergency circumstances is to send the brigade-sized *Groupement Aeroporte*, which is based at Albi and manned by regulars. Transport for the French paras is

provided by 70 C-160 Transall aircraft of the French Air Force, so once again airlift is a big problem.

France's Airborne Forces gained a reputation for uncompromising soldiering during the Indochina campaign of the late 1940s and early 1950s, and later in Algeria. But a putsch during the latter conflict led to them being treated with suspicion by successive French governments, and a restriction has since been placed on the amount of time an officer can serve with the Airborne Forces.

Influenced early on by the British Army, the Israelis wear the Red Beret

A chapter on the Airborne Brotherhood would not be complete without a mention of the Israeli paras. There are six parachute brigades all told (three regular, three reserve), and their role is to act as the spearhead of the Israeli Defence Forces (IDF). The period of basic training for Israeli paras is, at six months, comparable in length to that of the British Paras and, having been influenced early on by the British Army, they also wear the Red Beret.

The Israeli paras have taken part in some memorable actions in the various rounds of the Arab-Israeli conflict, including an airdrop on the Mitla Pass in 1956, the battle for Jerusalem in 1967, and the breakout from Suez in 1973. More recently, they led the 1982 invasion of south Lebanon, going in as an Airmobile trouble-shooting force in CH-53 helicopters. They can also mount Out-of-Area operations, as in July 1976, when an airlanded force of paras, along with men of the crack Golani Brigade, rescued over 100 Israeli hostages at Entebbe in Uganda.

The bond of mutual respect that is the Airborne Brotherhood

These days, the IDF uses a high proportion of Israeli-made equipment. Of this, the paras have the 5.56mm Galil assault rifle, the B-300 82mm rocket launcher, the Soltam lightweight 'Commando' 60mm mortar, and they can be ferried around in Israeli-made versions of the Sikorsky CH-53. And although the Israelis have 21 C-130 Hercules and 19 C-47 aircraft which provide a parachute option, it is as heliborne and mechanised crack infantry that their paras are most in demand today.

The success of paras around the world in adapting to helicopters and mechanised warfare has shown their flexibility, and their success as crack infantry has proved their determination and aggression in battle. These attributes set the Airborne Soldier apart from the rest of his army. All this, and the risks of parachuting, builds a bond between men of like character — the bond of mutual respect that is the Airborne Brotherhood.

CH-53Gs of the _Heeresflieger_ (German Army air corps) coming in to redeploy _Fallschirmjaeger_ to counter another armoured thrust during an exercise. The German Army operates 105 of these heavy-lift support helicopters, each of which can carry 64 troops, or 10,886 kg of cargo. in contrast, the British Army has to rely on the RAF to provide it with support helicopters.

THE REGIMENT AT WAR

In the final analysis, the true test of any soldier comes in the white-hot arena of battle, when the bullets are flying and his life is on the line. From the bitter street fighting of Arnhem, to the Falklands campaign of 1982, the men of The Parachute Regiment have proved themselves to be some of the finest and most formidable fighting troops in the world.

Ever since the creation of Airborne Forces, The Parachute Regiment has established a reputation for fighting ability that is second to none; a tradition of fulfilling the mission — whatever the cost. Since its very first operation — Operation Colossus, in which just seven officers and 31 other ranks attacked the Tragino Aqueduct in Italy in February 1941 — the Regiment has displayed all the traditional Airborne attributes on the battlefield.

In Operation Biting, the daring raid at Bruneval on the French coast in February 1942, for example, C Company

World War II Paras prepare for a training jump. Until the late 1950s, British Paras did not jump with a reserve 'chute.

A Parachute Regiment soldier with a 9mm Sten Mk II sub-machine gun and wearing standard British Army battledress. The classic Denison smock was introduced in 1942.

2 PARA captured a top secret radar set and two German radar experts. This in spite of the fact that C Company was but newly formed, the men had only barely finished parachute training, and had to cope with numerous enemy pillboxes and machine-gun posts.

However, the Regiment really established its reputation for fighting ability in North Africa, as part of the Allied army that landed in Morocco and Algeria in Operation Torch in November 1942 and advanced eastwards on Tunisia. Battalions from the Regiment were dropped and instructed to capture important airfields and road junctions ahead of the ground forces, which would then link up and relieve them — the classic airborne role.

In two out of the three operations, the advancing main body quickly relieved the airborne troops but, in the third, unexpected opposition halted the ground forces. The men of 2 PARA then found themselves 50 miles behind enemy lines and, after an epic two-day march under continual attack by aircraft, tanks and infantry, succeeded in reaching the Allied lines for the loss of three quarters of their original strength — a fine demonstration of the need for determination in the Regiment.

For the rest of the campaign, the three battalions fought in the ground role. They captured 3500 prisoners and inflicted over 5000 casualties, but their own losses were also extremely heavy: out of an original strength of 2000 men, fully 1700 were either killed or wounded. The fearsome reputation of the Regiment was such that, in one defensive battle, one parachute battalion was warned to expect 10 enemy battalions supported by 100 tanks.

The Paras were undaunted, however, and such was their ferocity and aggression that the awestruck enemy dubbed them 'The Red Devils'.

In 1943, the Regiment again excelled itself in the defence of Primosole Bridge in Sicily. Partly due to inaccurate 'drops', only 295 of the 1856 men of the 1st Parachute Brigade were on hand to carry out the operation, yet they still managed to capture the bridge and hold it throughout a day of fierce fighting against vastly superior numbers. The inaccuracy of the drops in this mission convinced 6th Airborne Division of the need for a special Pathfinder squadron, which would land in advance of the main force and mark out easily identifiable DZs.

'The Hun thinks only a bloody fool will go there. That's why we're going'

The Parachute Regiment also played a leading role in 'D-Day' — the Allied invasion of Normandy. By the time the first troops came ashore, the six parachute battalions had already fought many tough battles. One of their most notable actions was the attack on the Merville Battery. This was ringed by minefields and rows of barbed wire, defended by artillery and numerous machine guns, and manned by 180-200 men. As Major-General Richard Gale,

GOC 6th Airborne Division, said: 'The Hun thinks only a bloody fool will go there. That's why we're going.'

After landing, the CO of 9 PARA could only muster 150 of the 635 members of his battalion, the rest having been dropped wide of the DZ. Yet in spite of this, and the fact that the Paras had only one machine gun between them, the attack went ahead. With luminous skull-and-crossbones painted on their jackets, the Paras breached the defences and, in bitter hand-to-hand fighting, killed or wounded all but 20 of the enemy, who surrendered. Though it lost 70 men killed or wounded, the battalion succeeded in getting through to the guns. The 6th Airborne Division was extremely successful in Normandy, and achieved every objective it had been tasked with.

The Regiment is best remembered, however, for its heroic part in the bloody battle of Arnhem in September 1944. The 1st Airborne Division was tasked to capture the road bridge over the Lower Rhine and hold it for 48 hours. It was to prove, however, in Lieutenant-General Browning's immortal phrase, 'A bridge too far'.

The operation went wrong from the outset. A shortage

A 1 PARA mortar crew in action at Arnhem, near the Oosterbeek church. The almost-vertical mortar tube shows the close range of the fighting.

Two dead Airborne Soldiers collected by the Germans after the battle of Arnhem. The 1st Airborne Division lost 7134 killed or missing in the bitter fighting against II SS Pz Corps.

what was left of 1st Airborne Division pulled back across the Rhine; only 2163 out of the original 10,095 men made it back. As one of the survivors put it: 'We did all we could — but it wasn't bloody well possible.'

Since the war, The Parachute Regiment has taken part in numerous peace-keeping and counter-insurgency operations around the world, from Java and the bitter campaign in Palestine in 1945-48, to Northern Ireland.

In 1956, for example, the Regiment played a major role in the Suez crisis. On 5th November, Operation Musketeer saw 3 PARA jumping onto a 'hot' DZ on El Gamil airfield. Though it had little support or specialised equipment, and was faced by a numerous enemy backed by armour, assault guns, mortars and machine guns, the battalion rapidly captured all its objectives — seizing the airfield and dominating the beaches to allow the sea-borne force to come ashore unhindered the following day. The campaign was brief — the British and French forces withdrew for political reasons a week after landing — but the officers and men of the Regiment displayed all the qualities that their forerunners had in the past.

Eight years later, in the Radfan in 1964, 3 PARA overcome mountainous terrain, a brutal climate, and the fierce local tribesmen. Once more, controlled aggression paid dividends when the bullets started flying.

'It was just like all the training. I found that extremely comforting'

In 1982, the Falklands conflict once more proved that Parachute Regiment selection and training works. After six weeks at sea, 2 and 3 PARA went ashore at San Carlos and Port San Carlos. When they moved out of the beach-head, both proved the value of the hard training and miles of 'tabbing' that go to make the Regiment one of the fittest in the world.

In the north of East Falkland, for example, 3 PARA walked right across the island, and then fought the battle of Mount Longdon. In the south, 2 PARA fought the battle of Darwin and Goose Green, and then went north to fight for Wireless Ridge. Most of the men carried about 35kg, and some up to 50kg. The signals platoon sergeant of 2 PARA in the Falklands had one of the heaviest bergens:

'I couldn't pick it up because of the three spare batteries. Well, each of those f—ing batteries weighs six pounds, and I had three normal and three spare, and so the only way I could get the bergen on was to sit on the floor, put it on, and then two blokes pulled me up.'

However, while training and exercises prepared the Regiment to walk long distances with heavy weights, none of the officers or men had ever taken part in a live-firing battalion attack where the 'targets' were trying to kill them. In fact, the British Army had not carried out

of transport aircraft — a deficiency in British airborne capability that still holds true today — meant that only half the designated task force could be dropped on the first day, and then the arrival of the remaining troops was delayed by bad weather until too late in the battle. Also, due to poor intelligence, the Airborne Soldiers found themselves up against far more formidable defences than they were led to believe, including an élite SS Panzer Corps.

Eventually, only about 700 men succeeded in fighting through to the bridge. With courage and grim determination, this force held off tank and infantry attacks for three days and four nights, before the Airborne Soldiers were forced out of the burning houses they were defending. After a gallant but unsuccessful counter-attack, the 50 survivors who were not wounded chose to disperse rather than surrender. The remnants of the division were then forced onto the defensive on the outskirts of Arnhem.

Many of the German troops, hardened veterans of Normandy and the Eastern Front, later described the bitter, close-quarter fighting as the fiercest they had ever encountered. However, nine days after the initial landing,

such an attack for 18 years. A platoon commander from 3 PARA describes going into battle for the first time:

'The overwhelming feeling I had as we set off at last light was that this move forward to the start line was just like all the others I had done. Somehow, one expects "the real thing" to be different — background music, credits for the cast, something — but there was nothing. It was just like all the training. I found that extremely comforting.'

Even during the battle, the overwhelming feeling was that it was very similar to what everyone had practised, as a section commander with 3 PARA describes:

'It was very, very similar to training for battle. I think the only thing you don't get [in training] is the momentum of actually doing an attack; [on exercise] everybody is up there charging about like f—ing headless wonders. In the actual situation, with people firing back at you, people think. They actually look at a piece of cover and say, "That's not going to protect me", so they go somewhere else, whereas in training you can dive down and think, "Well, be alright here", because you can't be killed by a blank. If you are actually in a battle, you think, "Well, if I do draw fire here I will be in the s—t".'

A member of the SF platoon from 3 PARA describes how it all seemed like an exercise, '...until we got opened up on by the enemy machine guns and there were actually dead guys around us. Then, all of a sudden, it becomes a personal challenge — them and you. And if you don't get the fire down, then you are going to lose. It's like a tennis game: when the ball comes into your court you have to get it out again, and this was the same sort of thing. They were firing down onto our positions and they were winning at that specific moment, because they had

A Vickers machine gun crew of 1 Para Bde training in North Africa just before the Oudna operation in November 1942. Note the two water bottles carried by the nearest Para.

the initiative. It took a while, but when we did manage to put more firepower down onto them, we started to realise that when the blokes see the fire stop coming from their side, their morale goes down, especially when they see a lot of tracer. The book tells us to fire at 100 rounds [a minute] normal and 200 rounds [a minute] rapid. But, when the world is coming down on you, you press the trigger and don't let go — you fire as much as you possibly can.'

A section commander with 3 PARA on Mount Longdon describes his reaction to coming under effective enemy fire for the first time: 'With your first initial contact, all you want to do is get the f— out of the place. What happens, though, is you just lie there, until the commander makes a decision and says, "Let's do this".'

The controlled aggression required to pass 'P'

Britain's Airborne Forces often went into battle by glider during WWII. Here, reinforcements of 6th Airborne Division prepare to cross the Channel to Normandy on 7th June 1944.

Company comes out when Parachute Regiment soldiers come under fire. The 3 PARA section commander again:

'You don't have to tell them to keep firing. They just get on with it, even if they can't see the target. Some people say, "What a waste of ammo". But what can you do? You wouldn't just lie behind a rock, would you? You have to take the offensive, and the only way to do that is by using maximum weight of fire.'

But that aggression has to be controlled. For, not until the section commander gives the order to take cover can a rifleman dash down and crawl behind a rock to engage the enemy, as a section commander from 3 PARA relates:

'The first part of coming under fire was being engaged by a machine gun. It started spewing tracer and everybody went, "Oh, look at that". It was pretty — red and blue. Nobody dove to the ground, saying "Phew, f—ing hell". There was none of that.

'What you didn't realise was that, between each tracer, another five rounds were coming in your general direc-

tion; but you couldn't see them — only the tracer. Then you hear it actually hitting the ground in front of you. But again the system saves you; you only take cover on the commander's decision, and as I advanced up the hill, I didn't think it was worth taking cover 'cos I would have just lain there all day, though of course with a better chance of getting shot. So I just continued to advance.'

The series of steps that a section must take during the advance are taught as the six 'section battle drills' — preparation for battle, reaction to effective enemy fire, locating the enemy, winning the firefight, the attack itself and, finally, reorganisation. These drills utilise and modify the soldier's instinctive reactions, as a corporal with A Company 3 PARA on Mount Longdon describes:

'The battle drills are there and they work. Taking cover, for example. You would automatically crawl into a piece of cover anyway, certainly if you thought someone was going to shoot at you — it's a natural process. It's like anything. If somebody is throwing golf balls at you, you wouldn't stand up and try and catch them. You would go and hide, wouldn't you? And that is how we work.'

'We just took cover, located the enemy, and started winning the firefight'

If a drill isn't natural, then it must become instinctive, for there are few second chances for men who forget their drills when under fire. Sometimes, however, a man is lucky. The section commander describes one such second chance:

'A bloke was getting over the top of a rock and the magazine fell off his weapon, and so he went in with only one round up the spout, not realising there was no magazine on his weapon. But there is actually a drill: you are taught to check your magazine. After he fired the first round, he went to fire again and obviously realised, but too late, no magazine. Well, it was a total shock; from then on I imagine he went through life thinking: "If I ever have to do that again, I will put a fresh magazine on."'

In general, however, those drills *had* become instinctive throughout both battalions, which is one reason why 2 and 3 PARA were so effective. A platoon commander from A Company 2 PARA describes what happened when he came under fire at Goose Green:

'The enemy fire started as we were crossing open ground. When we got opened up on, we went hell for leather for the gorse line, about 100 yards to the front at that point. At the end, we were on flat ground, completely open. We just took cover, located the enemy, and started winning the firefight. Everything you have ever been taught is just second nature and it takes over and you start to do the job. You don't have time to think about whether you are going to get killed or injured or anything else. Those drills are the basis of any attack — they must work,

Suez 1956: 3 PARA lands on a 'hot' DZ on El Gamil airfield
Top: The CO with his radio operator and bodyguard move off.
Bottom: The airfield captured, 3 PARA prepares to advance.

and they do work. They are such basic drills as well. If you are going to win the battle, you have to find out where the enemy are. Anyone being fired on is going to want to know where it is coming from, if for no other reason than to know to run in the opposite direction.'

As for actually winning the firefight: 'You don't just sit there and pop rounds off until they have got their heads down. Whilst trying to pin them down you are working your way forward. Then, fingers crossed, they'll surrender.

'When you win the firefight, the enemy has gone. Very few people are going to continue fighting when they can't fire back at you because, when you have effectively won the firefight, people *can't* actually fire back at you.

3 PARA in the Radfan, 1964. Above: A 3.5" Rocket Launcher in action — a potent weapon against the Arab sangars. Right: Firing a 3" mortar. The soft sand provides little support to the baseplate, leading to inaccurate shooting.

But this business of actually winning the firefight — "Right, now we are going to fight through the position" — yes, it will happen, of course it will. But, on the whole, you will find that the majority who can't fire back at you aren't interested in sitting there waiting for you to come along and lob something in — I know I wouldn't want to. Winning a firefight isn't a matter of just pinning them all down; winning a firefight is chipping away, trying to take trenches out as you win them.'

At Goose Green, 2 PARA found that working through positions is a much lengthier business in war than on exercise, as a section commander from 2 PARA describes:

'The whole Goose Green position was one big depth position. They [the British Army] have in-depth positions 50m or perhaps 100m at the most beyond the first positions [in training], and that is lovely on exercise, but realistically, as in the Falklands, you are talking about four or five miles in depth. There were trenches all the way.'

He goes on to describe his rate of advance through these positions as being '...not actually at a great pace; every now and again there would be an hour or so to try and find out what was going on. But, once it started, we just kept on going forward and tried to pin them down, then started thinking again about the next one.'

During actual combat, orders become much briefer than the 'battle orders' taught on exercise, as a platoon commander from A Company 2 PARA describes:

'Orders become a little more sketchy, very much: "I am going left flanking, far section follow me". It is *that* quick. Speed is important. In any attack you have to have momentum, speed, surprise: the quicker you can put them out of action, the better. Though obviously you mustn't do it too quickly, or you might do it wrong.'

Getting the balance right is important for, if a commander doesn't take time to appreciate the situation, then he probably will 'do it wrong'. A corporal from 2 PARA describes how he first came under fire at Goose Green:

'We heard the fire going on around us, but it didn't actually affect us until we got to the brow of the hill and my 2I/C was taken out. Then it was a matter of crawling forward, see the position, and a quick appreciation of how you are actually going to split the section up.

'It is all very well wanting to push forward all the time, but for the section commander, they are his boys and he is not going to cross a piece of ground just because the platoon commander says so; they are his responsibility. You need a minute to look at that piece of ground and consider.'

At such moments, a commander must use his experience and intelligence to decide how to overcome the problem. But, above all, he must be flexible. The section battle drills are a framework around which to build an attack, not a parade-ground movement. The performance of the Regiment in the Falklands showed that its emphasis on flexibility and initiative — both vital for an airborne assault — paid dividends in the 'gutter' fighting of the Falklands. An SNCO with 2 PARA describes how the attack '...varied from trench to trench. It is not a question of "this is what you do". You have to adapt to the situation. Sometimes you could use fire support to get in there. Sometimes, now and again, we had to use a MILAN [anti-tank missile] round on them, hitting the bunker, taking it out, and then charging and taking it. Hopefully, everyone in the bunker is dead by the time you assault it; if not, then you have to kill or be killed. It is not a thing you think about, you just get on and do it. It is only afterwards that you think, "Well, bloody hell".'

Although most of what had been taught worked, some of the tactics in Army training pamphlets were out of date at the time, which again required flexibility and 'applied common sense'. In particular, the pamphlets taught that a section of eight men should perform flanking attacks with the machine gun detached off to one side to provide fire support while the rest of the section assaulted. A section commander in 2 PARA gives his view of such tactics:

'Oh yes, that's all for magazines; you know: "I will put my gun group on high ground there and another here" — it sounds lovely, but it simply doesn't work like that. The only time you can really do a flanking attack is probably at battalion level, possibly at company level. But, in a battle situation, you just can't get up and say: "Right, fire support there, we are going to go left flanking". You can't do that because you have stuff [friendly troops] all around

A sentry on duty in the Radfan, 1964. He is manning a Light Role GPMG, with sights set at 800m, and watching an RAF Bristol Belvedere helicopter bring in supplies.

you and you can't just sort of decide to wheel off left and knock off your own men. It looks lovely in the books with all them arrows going round and that, but really, no...once you are in contact, you must keep on moving towards the objective, no sort of flanking attack.'

'Sometimes, you just have to tell the guys to go for it'

The nature of the ground up to the enemy position also demands a flexible approach. At Goose Green, the Argentine trenches were in open country with long, flat fields of fire and hardly any cover. This made them very difficult to attack. A section commander from 2 PARA tells how standard British tactics of one person or group moving while another fires were not always the answer:

'You will obviously try and keep moving by bounds — the old buddy-buddy system in their pairs [one man fires while his buddy moves] — but sometimes that is not advisable. Sometimes, you just have to tell the guys to go for it and keep their heads down, to get on the position and then do the business.

'You crawl forward a little bit. But, once you are within about 40 or 50 metres, then you have to move very fast just to get on that position, and fire as you are moving forward. Sometimes, it wasn't feasible to have one section down and firing and the other section moving forward being covered. If you were that close, then you just had to run and fire and hope for the best.'

'At the end of the day, you have to get them from A to B as soon and as safe as possible. If it is the safest way —

A 105mm L5 Pack Howitzer of 1 Para Light Battery RA in the Radfan, 1964. At 1310kg it was light enough to be moved by helicopter, though it only had a range of 10.5km.

lots of cover, etc. — then yes, ideally we would move nice and slowly. But on a billiard table you just can't do it. You have to get up and go for it and, as long as there is fire going down, the enemy will keep their heads down.'

He and his section (part of D Company) had to use that tactic four or five times at Goose Green, but for 3 PARA on Mount Longdon, the terrain, with its many rocks, gullies and mounds, provided far more cover. Over that sort of ground, you can afford to employ tactics as per the book, and move 'nice and slowly', as a section commander from A Company 3 PARA relates:

'Basically, we were crawling. There's no bravado when somebody is firing rockets, you just get on with basic drill, and basic drill is to crawl forward; there is nothing else you can do. You couldn't stand up because of the rocks, you would have fallen over or broken your ankle. Plus not knowing what was there anyway.'

However, it is one thing to know the tactics you want to apply; it is often quite a different matter actually applying them. Every soldier is taught the importance of

spreading out from the men on either side of him. That way, a burst of machine gun fire or an artillery or mortar round will cause the minimum of casualties. A section commander from D Company 2 PARA describes the difficulty he had in doing this:

'Everyone faces two fears at such times: fear of death, and fear of failure'

'Say you are trying to push men out further to the left or right. If they can't see you, they would be worried because they have lost sight of you, and once that happens they will not so much stop as want to drift in again. You get two men fighting through, they like to be close together. You tell them to split up more than 10 metres. They are still quite close at 10 metres but, even then, some of the younger lads found 10 metres too far to be away from their buddies. You had to constantly tell them, "Keep on pushing, push apart", because they wanted to stick together. It is psychological; they feel safer if there is someone else there. On their own they feel on their own.'

This herd instinct was due more to apprehension than outright fear. A platoon commander from 3 PARA: 'The boys didn't seem particularly afraid; no one spoke of it,

Northern Ireland, 1970, before the breakdown in relations between the military and the Roman Catholic community — which the Army had originally been sent in to protect.

and the jokes had been flying as normal before we set off. We all knew each other extremely well, and we knew we were as well-trained as we'd ever be. Everyone faces two fears at such times: fear of death, and fear of failure. For me, the major fear was of failure, of not being up to it, that lurking question: "How will I react under fire?" '

A platoon commander from 2 PARA answers that question: 'You don't feel frightened at the time; you do beforehand, when you know you are going to do an assault, or moving across open ground waiting to get a contact. Once you are in a contact or firefight, the fear goes and you get on and do the job.'

This officer's reaction was typical. A section commander in 3 PARA remembers his feelings, and those of his Toms: 'There was no feeling of fear, as such. Apprehension, certainly, but once they were actually in there doing what came naturally, which they had been taught for X amount of years, they just got on with it, and if in the end they die...I mean, I put me hand on my heart and thought: "It is something that was required".'

The Falklands showed the importance of training — hard and realistic training. For it was the tough, thorough

Men from 2 PARA just returned to their base at Bessbrook after a border patrol in 1973. They are well armed, with two GPMGs in the section rather than the usual one.

training of its carefully selected members that enabled the 'Maroon Machine' to do what it did 'Down South'.

The emphasis on thorough training to create instinctive reactions applies to the mental rigours of the 'combat appreciation' as well as the actions of the section battle drills. A platoon commander with 2 PARA at Goose Green describes coming under fire for the first time:

'You don't feel frightened. On reflection, you realise there is a tremendous adrenalin boost about it and you have a job to do, and you get on and do that job, and then the drills that you have been taught in training come naturally. Before you realise it, you are looking at the ground, the situation, with a view to solving the problem. But the first thing is to get yourself under cover.'

Platoon and section commanders also have an advantage in overcoming fear. A corporal from 2 PARA:

'I was lucky being a section commander, very lucky, because I had been able to occupy my mind all the time.

Warrenpoint, 27 August 1979. The first bomb exploded in the layby throwing a 4-ton truck into the central reservation. The second destroyed a gatehouse on the right of the road.

It was constantly working, as was the 2I/C's. Say we had a lull in the battle: we stopped, and I would be thinking of my next move, objective, or orders, whereas the soldier doesn't have to, and so he has too much time to actually think about the consequences of what is going to happen next, and so fear will obviously come into it. When the men actually stop during a small lull, then it is very difficult to get them back up and moving again. Sometimes you would actually be running up and down and picking people up and saying: "Get into it again". When it is going on they are OK, but as soon as you stop and they get down, then they don't want to get back up again.'

A platoon commander in B Company 3 PARA kept his men active to overcome their fear: 'It's the old thing of the mind being so busy thinking about all sorts of things that you don't really have time for fear. One noticed that in the soldiers particularly, because they were waiting for things to do and they loved being told what to do. Once

you are doing something your mind is blocked out, so we were desperately giving them jobs to do — "Go and collect more ammo! Go and carry that body down the hill!" — because it gave them something to think about and concentrate on rather than fear. Once you left a bloke for a while and he stayed under cover too long, then he found it harder to move. So the soldiers loved being given jobs to do.'

'I had two soldiers who had only arrived from Depot the week before'

Although men might find it hard to move out of a safe position because of fear, rarely did they find it hard to move because they were exhausted. A section commander from A Company 3 PARA explains why:

'We were on a high, you see. I suppose it is like smoking dope — you go right to the outer limits; you are never tired because the exhilaration takes you away. Everybody was exactly the same — hyper is the word, I suppose. A lot of my soldiers were quite old, but some were very, very young. I had two soldiers who had only arrived from Depot the week before. Then, when it came down to it,

there was only one person who said he didn't enjoy it; the rest thought they had actually enjoyed going into it.'

A young rifleman from 2 PARA explains why he enjoyed the battle, despite his fear: 'It is a weird sort of feeling. There is so much adrenalin and excitement, like being in a fast car. There is an element of danger there, but the excitement...you are loving it. You are not so out-and-out scared that you freeze; I didn't feel like that. The adrenalin was keeping you going.'

A corporal from 2 PARA describes how he felt after several nights with little sleep and 24 hours of fighting through four miles of positions at Goose Green: 'Knackered — but you don't sleep. You might nod off when you get a chance, but only for five or 10 minutes. You don't sleep, because your mind is racing all the time. Physically, you are shattered, and mentally, you are very, very tired; but your mind is alert and keeping your body going. Then, when it stops, you realise just how really tired you are, and there is obviously the emotional thing of great, sheer relief. Thinking about a friend you have lost, you are very emotional for about 10 or 15 minutes afterwards, until you get control, you know.'

For most of the men in the Falklands, sights of death

The effect of the first bomb, which was hidden in a farm trailer — hence the straw around the remains of the Bedford RL truck. The two bombs killed 16 members of 2 PARA.

and mutilation were another new experience with which to cope. A platoon commander with 2 PARA: 'When you are picking up your wounded and dead, the fear comes back more as a form of shock, the first time the soldiers come into contact with a big firefight.'

'The possibility of one's own imminent death became an everyday reality'

A platoon commander in B Company 3 PARA found his attitude to death changing, even before his first attack: 'Normally, death is something that happens somewhere else, with special places for the dying and the dead. However, we found that — with British ships being sunk, the SAS helicopter going down, seeing the crew dead and lying in San Carlos water — death became a normal part of life. The possibility of one's own imminent death became an everyday reality, and something one got used to. So, when the platoon set off for Longdon, we knew

that a few of us would die, but had accepted it as one of the realities of life we could do nothing about. So I didn't fear death in the way I'd expected, and indeed never did during the whole of that night. It seems a bit naive really; you are used to the idea of dying, you are mentally warmed up to it. The shock really came afterwards.'

That acceptance of death could happen before, during or after battle. A section commander tells of his experience in his first battle — Goose Green:

'You are fighting for your own survival and the survival of the battalion'

'Once the first man gets killed, then you know it is for real, and because you keep on pushing your body, at one stage you accept death itself. You *must* accept it, because you have seen people dying all round you. And then, when you have done that, you can never be the same person again, even when the conflict is over. Although it never happened to you, the fact that your mind has accepted that you might die means you will never be the same man again. I was a 32-year old section commander, and it took me a good two years to get it out of my system. But a young lad, 17, 18, 19 years of age, well, even today it isn't out of their system. I am

The Falklands, 1982. Above: 21 May, 3 PARA goes ashore at San Carlos from 'rubbish skips', as the LCVPs were known. Right: A 3 PARA GPMG gunner on Mount Longdon. He has fixed a water bottle pouch to the gun to hold the ammo belt.

noticing people today who have not recovered.'

While this acceptance of death might have made it difficult to return to everyday life when the conflict was over, it was good preparation for another battle. And, at Wireless Ridge, the battalion fought that second battle (2 PARA was, in fact, the only battalion to fight two full-scale actions during the campaign.) A platoon commander from A Company 2 PARA compares the two battles:

'Very different attacks, in many ways anyway, but as an individual you come to accept the circumstances that you are in. It is not quite "Queen and Country" at that point; you are fighting for your own survival and the survival of the battalion as well, and you come to accept the possibility of what could happen to you — you may not get back to England again or anything else.

'Once you accept that, you settle down into the environment and become part of it. When we attacked Wireless Ridge, the soldiers had completely come to terms with it — "If it has my name on it, it has my name on it". So everything calms down and it isn't a rush, and

you are able to make decisions more easily. It is a much better attack as a whole, the second time around; people are more relaxed.

'They performed very well at Goose Green, don't get me wrong, but at Wireless Ridge, in the event of anything happening — either expected or out of the ordinary — they would have coped with it a lot better. There was probably more aggression on Wireless Ridge than at Goose Green; they had accepted what might happen to them so they got on with more aggression and did the job.'

This confidence and sureness of touch led to him getting far more professional satisfaction from a job well done, with the minimum of friendly casualties, and as part of a team working well together. In a strange way, this led him to enjoy the battle: 'You didn't laugh and joke and say "Well, isn't this great fun?" But it was a much better-orchestrated attack on Wireless Ridge, and there was more fire support. People were more confident about what they were doing, and that was the main thing.'

'It was a gateway to Stanley, and they all knew that was the last push'

Goose Green had brought home the reality of war to 2 PARA. A section commander in D Company explains how, for him, this had a beneficial effect:

'You knew what to expect. It is not an exercise any more; at Goose Green, blokes started dying. Carrying corpses back and all that, it hits you; so, the second time round, I was thinking: "Well, I will give this some more thought". I had lost a man already, within about two minutes of our first contact [at Goose Green]. I didn't plan to lose any more, so I thought a little more about what I was going to do. But, when you go up a rise, you have to push somebody up there first of all to cover you across, you can't just go bundling up a hill and not have any form of support at all. So [at Goose Green] I decided to push my 2I/C up with the gun so he could cover us, but as he went up over the hill, there was an enemy position there within four or five metres. So, he had a weapon and they were firing as well and he caught one in the eye — and that was it. But we still took that position.'

His emotions the second time round were different: 'At Goose Green, I wasn't scared — hyped up, obviously — but the real fear didn't hit me at all in that battle. It was a harder battle than Wireless Ridge, where not so much fear but a lot of apprehension came in. A lot more thought went into my plan. "It's your job to clear that area

Top: A Tom from 3 PARA escorting Argentine prisoners to the rear after the battle of Mount Longdon.
Bottom: A casualty is taken from a Scout helicopter to 2 PARA's RAP after the bombing at Bluff Cove.

there", I was told, and there was a lot more thought going into the details, and I had a lot more time for that, which is good; obviously, the longer you get, the better the situation you are going to be in. Whereas at Goose Green, it was a case of: there is a trench there and you have to make a quick decision and attack and go for it. And you just live or die by that quick reaction.'

Besides more time for planning and orders, the battalion also had more fire support at Wireless Ridge than at Goose Green. In the first battle, it was only three 105mm Light Guns, two 81mm mortars with insufficient ammunition, and the 4.5-inch gun of HMS *Arrow*, which jammed. For 'round two' there were 12 105mm Light Guns, the 4.5-inch gun of HMS *Ambuscade*, two Scimitar and two Scorpion light tanks, armed respectively with 76mm and 30mm cannon and machine guns, all 16 mortars of both 2 and 3 PARA, and the MILAN and machine-gun platoons of both battalions. In the words of a member of 2 PARA: 'There was more fire on Wireless Ridge, a lot more, and it made a big difference. It was a gateway to Stanley, and they all knew that was the last push.'

Goose Green showed that The Parachute Regiment could win a battle almost single-handed. Wireless Ridge showed that it realised the value of 'all-arms co-operation', of fire support in the 'combined arms assault'. Fire support effectively won the battle by suppressing or destroying the enemy positions, thereby allowing the rifle companies to get close enough to clear and secure the trenches. One of 3 PARA's machine gun platoons watched the bombardment of 2 PARA's first objective at the foot of Wireless Ridge and describes the effect on the Argentinians further up the slope:

'They were frightened to death after what they had just seen; the whole world went down onto that bottom part of the ridge with 2 PARA. When you are advancing, you have to have a firebase putting down sustained fire all the time. Accurate, so they keep their heads down while you get on top of them, get in amongst them.'

'It wasn't hand-to-hand fighting, just a load of corpses there, splattered'

And this was exactly what happened. A rifleman and his company '..advanced 'til we were virtually on top of them. The first [phase of the attack] was at night, and I didn't know how close they were. Also, we were in their positions [before they opened fire], which was a good thing — we literally fell in a trench and there we were.'

However, even the massive firepower did not destroy every Argentine position. A number of machine guns in well-constructed bunkers continued firing despite the suppressive fire and had to be dealt with by grenade and bayonet. This close-quarter combat was rare, though, as 'the positions were in bits. It wasn't hand-to-hand fighting, just a load of corpses there, splattered.'

When they did find an occupant, he did not last long: 'The bloke was half dead anyway really, just put up a sort of mediocre resistance, and I had to get rid of a lot of anger inside me and he just happened to be the unlucky person on the day, really.'

Once they had captured Wireless Ridge, D Company 2 PARA were then hit by the only Argentine counter-attack of the campaign. As one section commander remembers it:

'It wasn't really a counter-attack as in the book, it was more a sort of half-hearted attempt. But it *was* their airborne — nowhere near as professional as the British Army, of course, but pretty good. It was hairy and scary. It could have been quite serious, since they could have broken through the first section and then they would actually have been in amongst HQ, and it would have been difficult to keep control. But there were other [Para] sections moving down to the left, and they just started laying fire down, and that was basically enough for [the Argentinians] and they didn't want to know any more. They fell back down the hill again.'

'Then the fire started coming and you just had to take cover'

To be on the receiving end of an attack was a novel experience for the men of D Company, but it didn't bother that corporal at all:

'At least I knew that I was there in cover, and they were coming at me and I had rounds on me, lots of rounds, and I could just sit there all day popping them off. [At Goose Green] the defensive positions were taken after 14 hours, continuous fighting all the way. It was bloody knackering. I would rather be in the defensive position than have to do that.'

Besides the novel experience of attacking live targets, and of one company defending against a real assault, the men of 2 and 3 PARA also discovered what it was like to come under artillery fire. In particular, 3 PARA suffered considerable shelling after it had taken Mount Longdon:

'We were A Company at the time, and everybody was having a good look at the dead and that sort of thing, and then the fire started coming and you just had to take cover. At first it wasn't that accurate, but later on it started getting pretty close. We were lucky with a lot of the ammo — there were a lot of blinds. There was also the soft terrain; a lot of ammo didn't go off when it hit the peat.' (The damp peat also absorbed the impact of the shells and reduced the killing power of the splinters.)

There is not much an infantryman can do against artillery fire, other than protect himself from its effects — dig a trench and provide it with overhead cover. This impotence can be particularly frustrating for aggressive troops such as the men of The Parachute Regiment. They would rather be in a firefight where they can get at the guy shooting at them and do the business on him. A Falklands veteran tells of his experience:

'A lot of it was indiscriminate, and what do you do about it? You can't fight it, so you just have to sit there. You start to think, "Well, one has to come in sooner or later". God knows what it was like lying in a trench [during World War I], 10 days of artillery f——ing going in on you. But it is indiscriminate, and you start to anticipate: "It has been going over the mountain for the last day and a half, it must be coming further forward now". Then you hear firing in the distance and you think, "S——t, here they come again", so you are constantly on your guard.'

Being in an artillery impact area for such a long time can sap morale, so the officers and NCOs have to go round the positions and keep their soldier's spirits up. A platoon sergeant from C Company 3 PARA describes some of the factors which affected the men's morale, factors which tend not to come out on exercise:

'An interesting thing was the mail. We didn't really get much mail in the Falklands and, on one particular occasion, I received 10 letters, all from my wife, which she had written in about five days, two letters a day. When the mail arrived, because I was responsible for administration and discipline within the platoon, it was my job to go and pick up the mail for the company and distribute it. My signaller hadn't had any mail and he was a bit cut up about it, and in fact he started to cry, which I thought was very strange at the time, but then I realised that here he was in the middle of nowhere and nobody was bothering to write a letter to him. So, I gave him some of mine to read. And I didn't realise until that day how important cigarettes and mail really are. From that day on I always had, not so many letters, but about 800 cigarettes in my bergen at any one time so that I could throw out a packet to a bloke as a good morale booster, if nothing else. The fact that it was probably killing him slowly is neither here nor there.'

'You have to accept your losses at the end of the day'

Such was the morale-boosting effect of cigarettes that even non-smokers started to take up the habit, as the platoon sergeant describes: 'I had 25 men in the platoon; 15 were smokers when we went down there and I think 23 were smokers by the time we finished.'

It was not only factors affecting morale that came out in the Falklands after failing to appear on exercises. For example, the effect of coming under fire from a sniper was, perhaps, not fully appreciated until the 'real thing'. One section commander from 2 PARA found it:

'..worrying, to say the least, because you didn't know where the sniper fire was coming from. There was so much fire going on you couldn't pin-point the position. Men tried to get up over the rise, and there was a sniper just knocking them back. It was worse than machine guns; with a machine gun you know it is there and you know how to tackle it, because you can still get to a position where you can take it out. But a sniper was a different ball game. You had to try and keep going because the momentum must be kept going; you didn't want to keep stopping because there might have been a sniper there. If you lost one [member of your section] every now and again then I'm afraid that was just the way it had to be.

Men of C Company 3 PARA after their march into Stanley on 14 June 1982. The Argentinians surrendered rather than fight such determined troops in the Falklands' capital.

You have to accept your losses at the end of the day.'

However, if the losses in pushing forward become too great, even the most motivated of soldiers must stop and take cover. When a number of snipers pinned down his platoon, an officer with A Company 2 PARA fought a fire-fight for four and a half hours. Unable to advance, he was no longer achieving his mission:

'There were several snipers, and they could pin down a whole company. It is frustrating, because you can't get for-

Sgt Ian McKay of B Coy 3 PARA. He won a posthumous VC on Mount Longdon when he charged three machine guns pinning down his platoon, and destroyed them with grenades.

One of the most ruthless aspects of a sniper is the number of men he hits as they go in to help the first casualty. A platoon commander with B Company 3 PARA:

'Tragically, on returning, 1 Section fanned out, and their mortarman entered the area of a sniper, who shot him in the heel. The section commander ran in, only to be shot in the head — blinded. Then, a man from the peak [of Mount Longdon] leapt from cover and sprinted forward to help. I think he died before he hit the ground. More in horror than anything, I yelled: "Stop! No one's to go forward!" In one minute, a sniper had pinned down a section, leaving one dead, one dying and two with leg wounds that only the extreme cold prevented from being fatal, since it stopped the flow of blood.

'In two films on Vietnam since then, I have seen just this predicament portrayed. These films are far more instructive than any tuition I've ever received from Sandhurst or elsewhere. The callous cynicism of the sniper — that trades on one man's compassion for his fellow, and the urge to help the injured — demands an equally cold response, one that leaves the injured on their own until the sniper is dealt with. Having seen the carnage enacted in front of me, I ordered that no one would go forward until that sniper had been killed.'

'If you get a bit of shrapnel, then you get a bit of shrapnel'

There were many other lessons learnt — at Goose Green, on the slopes of Mount Longdon and on Wireless Ridge — that confirmed the principles and emphasis that the Regiment had long applied. One example was SF (sustained fire) machine guns (GPMGs mounted on tripods). The Falklands showed how effective they were, in attack as well as in defence. The Regiment had realised their value before the conflict, and each battalion had gathered extra guns to create a separate SF platoon. One of 3 PARA's SF platoon describes how powerful this grouping proved to be in the final phase of the battle for Longdon:

'In the morning, the battalion had regrouped, and there was A Company, ready to assault the far side. While they were waiting, we opened up with six guns. Daylight was just coming, and the whole company just got up and moved on to the ground — and they didn't have anything to do, just a few machine guns to deal with.'

Another weapon whose value showed itself in the Falklands was the '66' — a shoulder-fired, one-shot rocket intended for use against tanks and armoured vehicles. Used against Argentine bunkers and sangars (defensive positions constructed out of sandbags or rocks above ground level, where the ground is too hard to dig bunkers or trenches), the '66' had a considerable effect on the defenders — both physically and on their morale. But

ward and do things without taking casualties, and obviously you try and take the minimum amount of casualties; we are not in the game of mass frontal attack and human waste. For a start, we haven't got the people to do it with, and I don't think many soldiers would follow you if you said: "Right lads, line abreast and off we go!" But it is frustrating, because you try to find him. He is there causing you problems and you have got to get round it. If at first you don't succeed, try, try again. You try left and right flanking, and come back — whatever. You have to find a way round it, or find that person and get rid of him.'

it also has a tell-tale 'signature' — a lot of noise, smoke, and flash when it fires. A section commander with A Company 3 PARA on Mount Longdon describes how he learnt to modify the '66' firing drills:

'The second position we went into, I said "Right, get the '66s' out", and I wallied the '66s' into the position, thinking, "Well, this will give them a f___ing good hiding". And, of course, no sooner had I fired the '66s' than a .50 [calibre heavy machine gun] opened up in front of a rear position, 300 or 400 metres further back. So the drill was adopted that you fired the '66' and then went sideways as fast as you possibly could.'

Grenades can also be as dangerous to friendly forces as they are to the enemy. In the words of a section commander from D Company 2 PARA:

'You get little bits of shrapnel [from your own grenade], but that is just unlucky. You can't be too careful — you get too careful and you are on edge all the time. If you get a bit of shrapnel, then you get a bit of shrapnel; it is the name of the game.'

Perhaps the most reassuring aspect of the Falklands, though, is that the conflict showed just how good are the soldiers of The Parachute Regiment, that one of its greatest assets is the initiative and aggression of the individual Tom. Several times, attacks were led by private soldiers because their NCOs had been killed or wounded. A section commander with A Company 3 PARA describes one such occasion:

'Everyone has said it was the best exercise they had ever been on'

'One of my men, Sid Skunk and I, we were opened up on, and the force blew me off the rock — no flak or anything. Later on, we discovered that we had holes here, there and everywhere. The grenades blew us back over the wall and, by the time I had recovered, my soldiers were already in there and had dealt with it. So the loss of a commander was nothing. They went in there, bullets flying and everything else, and took the position out, and then they went further and just waited for me to recover. It was so quick; I went off the rock, Sid Skunk shouted "Let's take it out", and that is all I remember. The next thing, the soldiers were there, the mission had been accomplished and they were just waiting, re-charging their magazines as I walked over the rock, and all I got was, "Where have you been, you f—ing w—ker?" And that is just the way it goes.

'Everybody on top of that mountain [Mount Longdon] proved to everybody that the system works and that the standard of soldiers in The Parachute Regiment is far greater than anywhere else in the world, quite honestly.'

This self-confidence, and the many hard training exer-

Lt Col H Jones, the CO of 2 PARA until he died leading a gallant flanking attack on a machine gun position at Goose Green, for which he was awarded the Victoria Cross.

cises in the years before the conflict, is what enabled the Regiment to achieve such remarkable feats. In the words of a platoon sergeant from 3 PARA:

'Well, it has to be said that right from the word go, the Falklands didn't really come as any hardship to anybody in the battalion, because it was as good as a good exercise. Everybody has said it was the best exercise they had ever been on, and just took it from there. So, mentally and physically, to a certain extent we were quite well-prepared. There was quite a lot of live firing involved, and it was a two-way range.'

INTO THE 1990s

Ever since its creation, from the streets of Arnhem, through the 1945 demob, to the cuts of the 1970s, The Parachute Regiment has been battling for survival. But the enemy of tomorrow is not the Waffen SS or the Whitehall planners. It is a shortage of numbers. Though there will be far fewer young people, the Regiment needs to get more men of the same high quality — and keep them.

As British Airborne Forces go into their second 50 years, tension between East and West is decreasing, and operations to rescue hostages or assist a friendly nation in the Third World seem ever more likely than do massive armoured battles in West Germany. Since such 'Out of Area' operations are the speciality of 5 Airborne Brigade, the relative importance of The Parachute Regiment and Airborne Forces is increasing. So the future of the Regiment seems assured. But in what shape will it head towards the 21st Century?

In the early 1990s, the British Army faces an acute manpower crisis. The fall in the birth rate in the 1970s means that, by the mid-1990s, there will be a third fewer school leavers than in 1989. Not only will the different

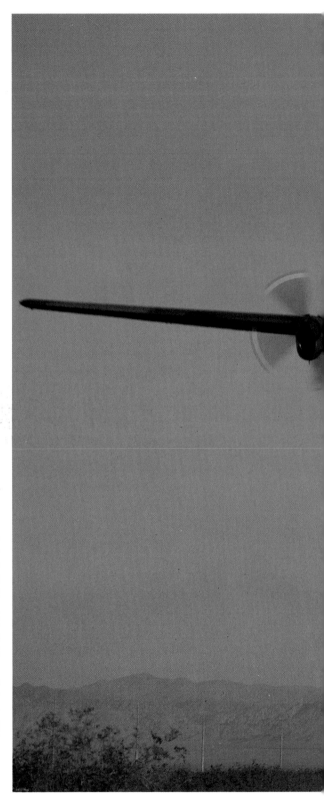

An RAF Hercules flies low over the African countryside. An operation to rescue British hostages in an unstable Third World country is far more likely than war in Central Europe.

A recruit at his pass-out parade. The flow of good quality young men into the Regiment must continue in the 1990s.

regiments, corps and Armed Forces be competing for the smaller number of young people, but so will commerce and industry — who can usually offer better salaries. Even in the last few years of the 1980s, some infantry battalions were suffering from a grave manpower shortage.

The Parachute Regiment is not immune from this problem. As one officer from the Depot puts it: 'Although enough of the *quantity* is coming forward, there's not enough of the right *quality*. And so, even though by comparison with the rest of the infantry The Parachute Regiment is well recruited, it's not up to full strength.'

In 1989, there was even speculation on whether one of the three battalions would have to be disbanded to make up the numbers for the other two 'in-role' battalions. Yet in a way, this is approaching the problem from the wrong angle. With today's emphasis on Out of Area operations, the Regiment has to get bigger, not smaller. Even when a battalion is not 'in-role', it still maintains its parachute capability. If something went drastically wrong on a 5 Airborne Brigade operation, then the 'out-of-role' battalion could well have to reinforce the other two.

So the Regiment aims to increase the number of men getting through to the battalions. One way to do this would be to have more men enter Depot to start training with each new recruit platoon. But there is a strict limit on numbers in each intake. This often causes frustration for those who want to join the Regiment, but have to wait up to a year before they can do so. Many are so keen to join the Army that they are persuaded to join some other regiment or corps, one which they can join immediately, rather than have to wait.

So, as the number entering Depot cannot be increased without the go-ahead of the MOD, the other alternative is to increase the percentage that pass through recruit training. As only 33 per cent of those who enter Depot as recruits pass 'P' Company, there is certainly scope for improvement in reducing the 'wastage'.

One solution would be to reduce the tough standards required to pass this gruelling test. But the Company Sergeant Major from Pegasus ('P') Company speaks for all the staff on that score: 'Certainly, there's no direct pressure on us to lower the standards, but sometimes it's implied. Luckily enough, we have managed to fight it off all the time. But there's always people trying to chip away at the system and we have got to resist change. I certainly resist changing 'P' Company as it is at the moment.'

However, the Recruit Company staff are also under tremendous pressure to get more 'Crows' through the system. Because 'P' Company is a separate testing organisation whose task is to maintain standards within Airborne Forces, it can resist any pressure that much better.

The Parachute Regiment is lengthening the time recruits spend in training

Any lowering of PPS standards would certainly cause resentment and disillusionment amongst those who have already passed it. They would feel that the regiment they joined no longer exists, that it was becoming just another 'ordinary' infantry regiment (where 98 per cent of recruits pass). The extra recruits admitted might not even make up for the increased number of trained soldiers who left. Giving the Red Beret to all and sundry in 5 Airborne Brigade already causes strong enough feelings within the Regiment (and the other elements of the Brigade who *have* earned it). A drop in standards would be even worse. As for those who might suggest that standards have *already* dropped, a field officer at Depot replies:

'I don't think standards have dropped, actually. People will say: "It was much tougher when I did it." I don't think this is true. I think that the standards today are as high, if not higher, than they have been in the past. Certainly, the course is much more technically orientated, and the standard expected in weapon training and fieldcraft and so on is probably of a higher standard than it was 10 or 15 years ago. I would suspect the only thing that has really changed is perhaps that the youth of today is a little bit softer than he was some years ago, but that's simply by virtue of the society he comes from.'

So the Regiment has sought to maintain standards, but increase the percentage passing 'P' Company in other

A section from 2 PARA armed with SA 80s. The Parachute Regiment battalions were among the first to receive the new weapon because of their high-readiness, Out of Area role.

fitness or robustness of even a few years ago. So to expect him to prepare mentally and physically for 'P' Company in the same time puts him under far more pressure than the recruit of the past. Depot needs longer to get him up to the same standard, because he starts at such a lower one.

Another advantage with the new system is that recruits will do their special-to-arm infantry training before the big test of 'P' Company. So those that fail and do not want to try again have already had a taste of infantry work and should be more inclined to transfer to another infantry regiment instead of leaving the army altogether. At present, about 50 per cent of those who drop out of Depot go back on the train to London as civilians.

The other way that the Regiment is cutting down on its wastage rate through Depot is through the PRAC (Pre-Recruit Assessment Course). As a Major at Depot describes it: 'It's really copied from an idea the Royal Marines have. They come down from the recruiting office and they spend two nights here with us, and in that time we are looking at them and they are looking at us. We try and sort out the sheep from the goats before we actually start. Otherwise, it's not in their interest to come down and then realise it's not what they wanted.'

And those that don't come up to the opening standards, or have their illusions about what it takes to be a paratrooper shattered, do not then come back again and waste Recruit Company's time, and valuable places. This will reduce the time a suitable potential recruit may have to wait to start Depot, so reducing the likelihood of him being persuaded to join another regiment .

'He had stress fractures in his feet, and he had to march 20 miles'

Some may well say that the particular regiment or corps he goes into does not matter, so long as he joins the Army he will make a good soldier. Yet when a soldier joins a regiment, he takes on its values and adopts the accepted pattern of behaviour within that regiment. An SNCO from 3 PARA describes the accepted behaviour in The Parachute Regiment:

'I have had soldiers who have been physical f—ing wrecks but been able to drag themselves up that little bit of extra hill just to make it to the top, 'cos that is all they want, you know. We had a classic example the other week: a fellow on the 20 miler. He had stress fractures in his feet, and he had to march 20 miles. He didn't know he had stress fractures, and he was in absolute agony. This guy made it to the end. Literally walking like a ballet dancer but he got there in the end. The proof of the pudding is there. He didn't want anyone to see him jack; he thought he would be letting his mates down, whereas in

An RAF Puma support helicopter prepares to lift a 105mm Light Gun in Norway. The helicopter is vital for moving artillery and artillery ammunition where there are few roads.

ways. For the pass rate of a test is not just a measure of its difficulty, but also how well the candidates have prepared for it. And so The Parachute Regiment is lengthening the time recruits spend in training. Instead of 24 weeks, basic training will last 27 weeks, and recruits will attempt 'P' Company relatively later, in weeks 19 and 20 instead of weeks 12 and 13. The Regiment has realised (or rather, made the powers that be realise) that today's new recruit, straight off the street, has nowhere near the

a different unit they wouldn't think twice about an excuse to get off it, that is the difference between us.

'It's the ribbing you get off the blokes that makes you go on. I mean, the other day, that jump we done on the airfield. A couple of blokes had little pains in the ankles and the odd little twists, but they would rather go and jump out of an aircraft and risk a more serious injury than stay back and take the ribbing off the blokes.'

'Airborne Forces are like a chain: it's as strong as the weakest link'

Yet this author has known soldiers complain at having to do long tabs and 10-mile speed marches when they were part of 5 Airborne Brigade in the airlanding role. 'Why should we do 10-milers, we aren't Paras?' was their line of argument, rather than: 'Paras do it, why can't we?' For an élite regiment can provide a benchmark against which a standard infantry battalion can measure itself — a target to beat. And, on occasions, some units, driven by regimental pride, have achieved this. The team from the Royal Hampshire Regiment, for example, managed to beat the team from The Royal Marines (and all those from

Left: Helicopters have only a limited range, and in many scenarios, parachuting is the only way of going in.
Right: Inside part of 5 Airborne Brigade's HQ, which is run by 5 Airborne Brigade's own HQ and Signals Squadron.

abroad) during the AFNORTH infantry competition in 1988.

Yet what makes The Parachute Regiment an élite is that every individual is of a high standard, and not just part of a small team. As one major described it: 'The Airborne Forces are rather like a chain: it's as strong as the weakest link. We are looking for a very high level of the lowest common denominator, and as long as the chain is strong enough for our purposes, then we reckon the chain, in other words the Regiment, is OK. Because, when you have 90 men in an aircraft and you get one weak man in there, it can upset the whole thing.'

So the supply of correctly motivated and determined young men must not be allowed to dry up. Enough recruits must somehow drag themselves through the pain of 'P' Company. Also, Toms must be persuaded to stay in the battalions after their first three years of service. As one CSM at Depot puts it: 'The name of the game is retaining soldiers. Without them, it is the end of the Regiment.'

5 AIRBORNE BRIGADE ORBAT

HQ 5 AIRBORNE BRIGADE
89 Int Section
Air Force Liaison Section
2 x Parachute Battalions
1 x Infantry Battalion
1 x Gurkha Battalion
Pathfinder Platoon
1 x Armoured Recce
 Regiment (Life Guards/
 Blues and Royals)
7 (Para) Regiment Royal
 Horse Artillery
36 Engineer Regiment Royal

Engineers, comprising:
9 (Para) Sqn
20 Field Sqn
50 Field Construction Sqn
61 Field Support Sqn
HQ & Signal Sqn Royal
 Signals
DET 224 Signal Sqn Royal
 Signals
658 Aviation Sqn Army Air
 Corps
613 Tactical Air Control
 Party RAF

614 Tactical Air Control
 Party RAF

LOGISTIC BATTALION
63 Sqn Royal Corps of
 Transport
82 Ordnance Company Royal
 Army Ordnance Corps
10 Field Workshop Royal
 Electrical and Mechanical
 Engineers

23 Parachute Field

Ambulance Royal Army
 Medical Corps
160 Company Royal Military
 Police

TA ENHANCEMENT
210 (V) Sqn Royal Corps of
 Transport
3 x General Service Units
163 (V) Company Royal
 Military Police

THE PARACHUTE REGIMENT

Formed: 1 August 1942

Headquarters: Browning Barracks,
Aldershot, Hampshire

Motto: *Utrinque Paratus* — 'Ready for
Anything'

Strength: approximately 3500 officers
and men

Regular Battalions: 3

1st Battalion (1 PARA)
2nd Battalion (2 PARA)
3rd Battalion (3 PARA)

Regular battalions recruit nationwide
and accept transferees from other
regiments and corps of the Army

TA Battalions: 3

4th Battalion (4 PARA)
(Lincolnshire and northern England)
10th Battalion (10 PARA)
(London and the Southeast)
15th Battalion (15 PARA)
(Scotland)

MAJOR OPERATIONS AND ACTIONS
OF THE PARACHUTE REGIMENT

1941
Feb 10/11 — Tragino Aqueduct:
Operation Colossus. 11th SAS Bn
(First British Airborne operation)

1942
Feb 27/28 — Bruneval: Operation
Biting. 2 PARA
Nov 12 — Bone Airfield. 3 PARA

1943
March 27 — Tamera. 1st Para Bde
July 13 — Primosole Bridge,
Sicily: Operation Marston. 1st Para Bde

1944
June 1 — Rimini, Italy: Operation Hasty.
6 PARA
June 6 — 'D' DAY (inc Pegasus Bridge
and Merville Battery). 6th AB Div
June 12 — Breville. 12 PARA
August 15 — Southern France:
Operation Dragoon. 2 Ind Para Bde

Sept 17-25 — Arnhem: Operation
Market Garden. 1st AB Div
Oct 12 — Megara, Greece: Operation
Manna. 4 PARA
Dec 24 — Ardennes. 6th AB Div

1945
Jan 3 — Bures, Ardennes. 13 PARA
March 24 — Rhine crossing: Operation
Varsity. 6th AB Div

1956
Jan-Dec — Cyprus (EOKA troubles). 16
Para Bde
Nov 5 — El Gamil Airfield: Operation
Musketeer. 3 PARA (Suez campaign)

1964
May — Radfan. 3 PARA

1965
March-June — Borneo. 2 PARA

1967
May 5-Nov 29 — Aden. 1 PARA
(1 PARA were the last unit out of Aden)

1969
March 19-Sept 14 — Anguilla:
Operation Sheepskin. 2 PARA
(2 PARA were awarded the Wilkinson
Sword of Peace)

1969 —
Northern Ireland: Operation Banner. 1,
2, and 3 PARA

1982
April 2-June 15 — Falkland Islands:
Operation Corporate. 5 Inf Bde (2, 3
PARA)

PARACHUTE REGIMENT BATTLE HONOURS

World War II

BRUNEVAL*
NORMANDY LANDINGS*
PEGASUS BRIDGE
MERVILLE BATTERY
BREVILLE*
DIVES CROSSING
LA TOUQUES CROSSING
ARNHEM 1944*
OURTHE
RHINE*
SOUTHERN FRANCE*
NORTHWEST EUROPE
  1942, 1944-45
SOUDIA
OUDNA*
DJEBEL AZZAG 1943
DJEBEL ALLILIGA
EL HADJEBA

TAMERA*
DJEBEL DAHRA
KEF EL DEBNA
NORTH AFRICA 1942-43
PRIMOSOLE BRIDGE*
SICILY 1943
TARANTO
ORSOGNA
ITALY 1943-44
ATHENS*
GREECE 1944-45

Falklands Campaign

GOOSE GREEN
MOUNT LONGDON
WIRELESS RIDGE

* Borne on the Queen's Colour

PARACHUTE REGIMENT VICTORIA CROSSES

World War II

Captain L. Queripel
10 PARA (Arnhem)*

Lieutenant J. Grayburn
2 PARA (Arnhem)*

Three other VCs were awarded to members of the Airborne Forces after the ill-fated Arnhem operation; two were to non-Parachute Regiment men of the 1st Airborne Division, and one was to an RAF pilot:

Major R.H. Cain South Staffs

Lance Sergeant J. Baskeyfield South Staffs*

Flight Lieutenant D. Lord RAF*

Falklands Campaign

Lieutenant Colonel H. Jones 2 PARA (Goose Green)*

Sergeant I. McKay 3 PARA (Mount Longdon)*

* Denotes posthumous award

PROGRAMME FOR THE TEST WEEK OF PRE-PARACHUTE SELECTION — 'P' COMPANY

ALDERSHOT PHASE

Day One a.m.

EVENT: Steeplechase.
TYPE: Individual.
COURSE: 2 x 1.3km circuit with obstacles.
DRESS: Shorts and boots.
TIME: 17.5 minutes for two circuits average.

EVENT: Log Race.
TYPE: Team (8-man).
COURSE: 2.8km.
DRESS: Helmets, PT vest, lightweights, boots, webbing (empty).
TIME: Average 12-14 minutes.

Day One p.m.

EVENT: Milling.
TYPE: Individual.
DESCRIPTION: Fighting, (boxing discouraged).
DRESS: PT kit with 16oz boxing gloves.
TIME: 1 minute's duration.

Day Two a.m.

EVENT: Speed March.
TYPE: Individual (soldiers march in squad).
COURSE: 16km.
DRESS: Boots, lightweights, combat jacket with 22kg load.
TIME: 1 hour 45 minutes.

EVENT: Confidence Course.
TYPE: Individual.
COURSE: Trainasium — 7-metre-high pathway with obstacles and 15-metre-high shuffle bars.
DRESS:Boots, lightweights, PT vest, helmet.
TIME: None. Soldiers must complete course to pass.

Day Two p.m.

EVENT: Assault Course.

TYPE: Individual.
COURSE: 3 x 400m circuit with 18 obstacles a lap.
DRESS: Boots, lightweights, PT vest, helmet, webbing (empty).
TIME: 7 minutes average.

BRECON PHASE (EXERCISE STEEL BAYONET)

Day Three

EVENT: Endurance March.
TYPE: Individual (soldiers march in squad).
COURSE: 28km.
DRESS: Boots, lightweights, combat jacket with 22kg load.
TIME: Four hours (with half-hour rest).

Day Four a.m.

EVENT: March.
TYPE: Individual.

COURSE: 15km (over Pen-y-Fan and Fan Fawr).
DRESS: As Endurance March.
TIME: About two hours.

Day Four p.m.

EVENT: Speed March.
TYPE: Individual.
COURSE: 10km.
DRESS: As Endurance March.
TIME: One hour and 6 minutes.

Day Five

EVENT: Stretcher Race.
TYPE: Team (12-man).
COURSE: 12km.
DRESS: As for the LogRrace — teams carry 80kg stretcher.
TIME: One hour and 20 minutes average.

'P' Company ends — Passes receive Red Berets

PROGRAMME FOR BASIC PARA

(Note: timings are approximate and depend on the students' progress)

Day 1 a.m. Opening address and documentation. Flight and Landing practice. p.m. PX1 Mk4 and Mk5 parachutes — demonstrations. PR7 reserve parachute — demonstration.

Day 2 a.m. Flight and Landing practice. Harness Release and Drag (HR&D) — introduction. Fan Descent Trainer — introduction. p.m. Jumping — introduction. Balloon descent — lecture.

Day 3 a.m. Tower — introduction. p.m. PX1 Mk5 — introduction. Fixed parachute and balloon car drill.

Day 4 a.m. Balloon descent. p.m. PX1 Mk4 — introduction. Fixed parachute and aircraft drill and exits.

Day 5 a.m. Flight and Landing practice. PX1 Mk4 — fitting. PR7 reserve — introduction. p.m. Exit drill. Fan Descent Trainer.

Day 6 a.m. Flight and Landing practice/Aircraft drill. p.m. Fan Descent Trainer. Lecture/film on aircraft drill.

Day 7 a.m. Flight and Landing practice. Standard and emergency aircraft drill. p.m. Parachute drill and air-experience flight (each student sees what it is like to stand in the door).

Day 8 a.m. Flight and Landing practice. HR&D. p.m. Aircraft exits and drill. Outdoor Exit Trainer — introduction.

Day 9 a.m. Flight and Landing practice/Aircraft drill. p.m. First aircraft descent in 'clean fatigues' (without equipment).

Day 10 a.m. Flight and Landing practice/Aircraft drill. p.m. Fan Descent Trainer.

Day 11 a.m. Second 'clean fatigue' aircraft descent. p.m. Descents with equipment — introduction.

Day 12 a.m. Flight and Landing practice. Packing containers — introduction. p.m. HR&D with equipment — introduction. Outdoor Exit Trainer.

Day 13 a.m. HR&D. Aircraft drill. p.m. Third 'clean fatigue' aircraft descent. Fourth (Night) aircraft descent.

Day 14 a.m. Flight and Landing practice/Aircraft drill. 'Service and stack' — introduction to container repacking and stowing on aircraft. p.m. Aircraft emergencies — film/lecture.

Day 15 a.m. Fifth aircraft descent — with equipment p.m. Flight and Landing practice/Aircraft drill.

Day 16 a.m. Flight and Landing practice. Container packing. Parachute Life Preserver (PLP) — introduction. p.m. Preparation of containers for parachute descent. Aircraft drill. Jumping with 'light scales' — lecture/demonstration.

Day 17 a.m. Flight and Landing practice/Aircraft drill. p.m. Sixth aircraft descent — with equipment. 'Service and stack.'

Day 18 a.m. Flight and Landing practice. p.m. Seventh aircraft descent — with equipment.

Day 19 a.m. Operational aircraft drill with live loads — introduction. 'Service and stack.' p.m. Eighth (Operational) aircraft descent.

Day 20 a.m. Dekit. Debrief.

p.m. Wings parade. Disperse.

GLOSSARY OF ABBREVIATIONS, TERMINOLOGY & SLANG

2I/C — Second-in-Command

2REP — *2e Regiment Etranger de Parachutistes*: 2nd Foreign Legion Parachute Regiment

AAC — Army Air Corps

AB — AirBorne

ABI — AirBorne Initiative

ACE Mobile Force — Allied Command Europe's Mobile Force

Advanced Wales — the Para recruits' 3-week military skills course

AFNORTH — Allied Forces NORTHern Europe

AFV — Armoured Fighting Vehicle

Airdrop — to drop by parachute

Airhead — a secure base in the target country through which resupply and reinforcement by air can take place

Airland — to deliver by landing from aircraft

Air-mounting — the organising of troops for delivery by air

AMF — further abbreviation of ACE Mobile Force

Ammunition boots — Army boots with studded leather soles (popular for drill)

APWT — Annual Personal Weapon Test

AST — Arctic Survival Training

AWT — Arctic Warfare Training

BAOR — British Army of the Rhine

Basic Para — basic static-line parachuting course

Basic Wales — week-long course of basic military skills taken early in training in the Brecon area

Battlecraft — the skills of a section or platoon working together as a team in battle

BDF — Belizean Defence Force

Bergen — a type of rucksack

BFA — Blank Firing Attachment

BFT — Basic Fitness Test

Blind — dud shell

BMA — Brigade Maintenance Area

Bull — 1. 'bullshit'; 2. to polish boots to a deep shine

Bundeswehr — Federal German Army

Cadre — 1: course; 2: staff (as in 'training cadre')

CAP — Company Aid Post

Casevac — Casualty evacuation

CEFO — Combat Equipment Fighting Order (see Fighting order)

Chalk — aircraft-load of troops (either parachuting or airlanding)

Clean fatigue — (of parachute jump) without equipment